COUNTER REALIGNMENT

In *Counter Realignment*, Howard L. Reiter and Jeffrey M. Stonecash analyze data from the early 1900s to the early 2000s to explain how the Republican Party lost the northeastern United States as a region of electoral support. Although the story of how the "Solid South" shifted from the Democratic Party to the Republican Party has received extensive consideration from political scientists, far less attention has been given to the erosion of support for Republicans in the Northeast. Reiter and Stonecash examine how the Republican Party lost as it repositioned itself, resulting in the shift of power in the Northeast from heavily Republican in 1900 to heavily Democratic in the 2000s.

Howard L. Reiter is Emeritus Professor of Political Science at the University of Connecticut, where he taught from 1974 to 2009 and was department head from 2003 until 2008. He specializes in American politics with a focus on political parties and elections. Professor Reiter is the author of *Selecting the President* and *Parties and Elections in Corporate America,* as well as book chapters and numerous articles in scholarly journals.

Jeffrey M. Stonecash is Maxwell Professor in the Maxwell School, Syracuse University. He does research on political parties and changes in their electoral bases. He has published *Class and Party in American Politics* (2000), *Diverging Parties* (2002), *Political Polling* (2003; 2008, second edition), *Parties Matter* (2006), *Governing New York State* (2006), *Split: Class and Cultural Divisions in American Politics* (2007), *Reassessing the Incumbency Effect* (Cambridge University Press, 2008), and *Dynamics of American Political Parties* (Cambridge University Press, 2009). He is currently working on a book about the relationship between presidential and House elections since 1900.

T0370638

To

Laura Reiter

Kathryn Edwards Stonecash

Counter Realignment

Political Change in the Northeastern United States

Howard L. Reiter

University of Connecticut

Jeffrey M. Stonecash

Syracuse University

CAMBRIDGE
UNIVERSITY PRESS

Shaftesbury Road, Cambridge CB2 8EA, United Kingdom

One Liberty Plaza, 20th Floor, New York, NY 10006, USA

477 Williamstown Road, Port Melbourne, VIC 3207, Australia

314–321, 3rd Floor, Plot 3, Splendor Forum, Jasola District Centre, New Delhi – 110025, India

103 Penang Road, #05–06/07, Visioncrest Commercial, Singapore 238467

Cambridge University Press is part of Cambridge University Press & Assessment,
a department of the University of Cambridge.

We share the University's mission to contribute to society through the pursuit of
education, learning and research at the highest international levels of excellence.

www.cambridge.org
Information on this title: www.cambridge.org/9780521186810

© Howard L. Reiter and Jeffrey M. Stonecash 2011

First published 2011

A catalogue record for this publication is available from the British Library

Library of Congress Cataloging-in-Publication data
Reiter, Howard L.
    Counter realignment : political change in the northeastern
    United States / Howard L. Reiter, Jeffrey M. Stonecash.
        p. cm.
    Includes bibliographical references and index.
    ISBN 978-0-521-76486-5 (hardback) – ISBN 978-0-521-18681-0 (pbk.)
    1. Republican Party (U.S. : 1854–) – History – 20th century.   2. Northeastern
    States – Politics and government – 20th century.   3. Political parties –
    Northeastern States – History – 20th century.   I. Stonecash, Jeffrey M.
    II. Title.
    JK2356.R29   2010
    324.27340974–dc22   2010030819

ISBN   978-0-521-76486-5   Hardback
ISBN   978-0-521-18681-0   Paperback

Contents

Figures

Tables

Preface

In recent decades, political science has made great strides in understanding the process by which parties and their leaders strategize to build new majority coalitions. Alongside traditional emphases on social and demographic changes and their partisan consequences – what we might call structural causes of political change – there is a new focus on deliberate strategies by party elites, an emphasis on agency.[1] This academic trend was inspired in part by the remarkable renewal of the Republican Party in the past half-century, and especially its extreme growth in the South.

Whereas much has been learned about such strategies, some aspects of these developments have not received adequate attention. Just as the perspective of the victors of wars tends to dominate the history books, ascendant parties enjoy special attention from parties' scholars. We have many books about the Republican surge in the South, but less research on where the party lost strength. This distortion has entailed underemphasis on certain parts of the country.

Our analysis is an attempt to correct these imbalances by examining the very important changes in the Northeast, the region where the Republicans have suffered the most over that same half-century. Almost in reverse correlation with Republican advances

---

[1] See, for example, D. Sunshine Hillygus and Todd G. Shields, *The Persuadable Voter: Wedge Issues in Presidential Campaigns* (Princeton, NJ: Princeton University Press, 2008); and David Karol, *Party Position Change in American Politics: Coalition Management* (New York: Cambridge University Press, 2010).

in the South have come Republican losses in the Northeast, which for much of the party's history was its strongest base. These developments can be attributed in part to demographic and social changes, often similar to those of the South but often distinctly northeastern, but also to the effects of deliberate strategies by party elites. Such prominent figures as Franklin D. Roosevelt, John F. Kennedy, Lyndon B. Johnson, Barry Goldwater, Richard M. Nixon, Ronald Reagan, and Newt Gingrich have helped cause titanic political changes in the Northeast, whereas their political adversaries have helped shape the outcome by their responses to these leaders' actions.

In this study, we take a historical approach to understand and explain these monumental changes. Many of the events and phenomena we discuss should be familiar to every student of American political history in the twentieth and twenty-first centuries – the New Deal, civil rights, the conservative reaction against the welfare state, and the response of social conservatives to the social upheaval that reached a crescendo in the 1960s. We will show that all of these developments helped drive the Northeast away from the Republican Party and toward its current Democratic status. More broadly, we hope to promote a better understanding of the dynamics of political change in America.

Howard L. Reiter
Jeffrey M. Stonecash

Acknowledgments

This book was first conceived at the State of the Parties Conference in 2005 at the University of Akron, and the authors are grateful to John Green, Director of the Ray C. Bliss Institute of Applied Politics, for hosting the conference and inviting us to participate. Earlier versions of portions of this book were presented to the 2007 annual meeting of the Social Science History Association, the 2008 annual meeting of the American Political Science Association, and the 2010 meeting of the New England Political Science Association. Useful feedback was provided at those meetings by John Berg, William Crotty, Kathleen Frankovic, Nolan McCarty, Nicole Mellow, Jerome Mileur, Arthur Paulson, Kent Redding, Peter Tammeveski, and Timothy Thurber.

Postscript: Democratic Fortunes in the Northeast in 2010

The years 2000 to 2008 witnessed a clear trend in the Northeast toward the Democratic Party. The elections of 2010 provided an indication of whether that trend could survive a national move to the Republicans. Republicans made some gains in the Northeast, but those elections also served to increase the region's difference from the rest of the nation because Republicans made much greater gains outside the Northeast. Although the rest of the nation moved decisively Republican in 2010, the Northeast remained heavily Democratic – despite the effect of Tea Party candidates who focused on the economic and budget issues that had been more popular in the Northeast than the social issues that Republicans often promoted.

The situation over the course of the decade is seen in the accompanying table. When the decade began, the Northeast was more supportive of Democrats. Democratic presidential candidates won a higher percentage of the vote in the Northeast, and Democrats won a higher percentage of Senate and House seats. By 2008, Democrats were doing better within the region for all offices. The 2010 national political conditions were very negative for Democrats. A strong majority saw the country as headed in the wrong direction, there was little national job growth, and the recently passed health care legislation was vehemently opposed by conservatives, who thought that the national government was becoming too big.

Year	Democratic support by Northeast and remainder of the nation					
	President vote %		% Senate seats		% House seats	
	Northeast	Remainder	Northeast	Remainder	Northeast	Remainder
2000	57.6	47.5	60.0	46.3	59.6	45.7
2002			60.0	45.0	58.3	44.7
2004	57.1	47.3	60.0	40.0	59.5	43.0
2006			75.0	45.0	73.8	48.3
2008	60.7	52.0	80.0	52.5	81.0	53.9
2010			75.0	47.5	67.9	38.5

The conditions were ripe for substantial Republican gains, and nationally they gained more than 60 seats in the House and 6 seats in the Senate.[1] Their gains in the Northeast, however, were more modest. In the House, outside the Northeast, Republicans gained 54 seats, moving from a 162–189 seat disadvantage to a 216–135 seat advantage. Their percentage of seats outside the Northeast increased from 46.2 to 61.5. In the Northeast they picked up 11 seats, moving from 19.1 percent of seats to 32.1. In the Senate, outside the Northeast, Republicans won 19 of 27 seats, while in the Northeast they won only two of the seven seats up for election.

The 2010 elections left the Northeast congressional delegation even more distinct in its partisanship from the rest of the nation. In 2000, the Northeast Senate delegation was more Democratic by 13.7 percentage points (60.0–46.3). After 2010 the difference was 27.5 percentage points (75.0–47.5). The House delegation also was more distinctly Democratic relative to the remainder of the nation. In 2000, the region was more Democratic by 13.9 percentage points, and by 2010 the region's delegation was more Democratic by 29.4 percentage points. The Northeast congressional delegations had become more Democratic across the decade and their difference in partisanship was greater than 10 years prior. The 2010 elections provided little indication that the region's drift away from Republicans was likely to slow.

---

[1] All results were as of November 8, 2010, based on CNN results and projections. Some results may have changed with recounts.

CHAPTER 1

Party Strategies and Transition
in the Northeast

Political parties are preoccupied with having majority status. When they are in the majority, they are often nervous about retaining power and continually search for new supporters. When they are in the minority, they seek to expand their electoral base. In both cases, a party seeks a strategy that will pull voters away from the other party. The strategy may be short term, as when candidates in a campaign try to use "wedge" issues to persuade voters attached to the other party to defect.[1] In 1964, President Lyndon Johnson, wanting to improve his support among blacks in northern cities, supported civil rights measures.[2] Other times, the strategy may involve a much longer-range plan. In the 1960s, Republicans sought gradually to move conservative Southerners away from the Democratic Party by expressing empathy with those angry about integration.[3] Later the party sought to increase its support among those with strong religious commitments by expressing opposition to abortion and homosexuals.[4]

---

[1] D. Sunshine Hillygus and Todd G. Shields, *The Persuadable Voter: Wedge Issues in Presidential Campaigns* (Princeton, NJ: Princeton University Press, 2008).
[2] Sidney M. Milkis, "Lyndon Johnson, the Great Society, and the Modern Presidency," in Sidney M. Milkis and Jerome M. Mileur, eds., *The Great Society and the High Tide of Liberalism* (Amherst, MA: University of Massachusetts Press, 2006), 1–49.
[3] Joseph Aistrup, *The Southern Strategy Revisited* (Lexington, KY: University of Kentucky Press, 1996).
[4] Geoffrey Layman, *The Great Divide: Religious and Cultural Conflict in American Party Politics* (New York: Columbia University Press, 2001).

The effectiveness of these strategies in moving voters from one party to the other has been of considerable fascination and has received substantial attention.[5]

These efforts, however, are not likely to be costless. Attracting one group of voters may alienate another. This possibility of losing voters, however, has often received less attention than strategies to gain voters. The plight of Democrats in the South has received the bulk of attention. The national party's increasing support for civil rights, particularly in the 1960s, alienated many conservative southern whites and provided the Republican Party with an opportunity to appeal to them.[6]

The negative consequences of Republican strategies have received considerably less attention. Indeed, the focus has largely been on the success of Republicans in using various issues to expand their electoral base.[7] Their strategies, however, have had some negative consequences. Some argue that their heavy emphasis on tax cuts has cost them support among those troubled by a lack of job growth and a volatile economy.[8] Others argue that the focus on conservative social issues and disdain for experts have alienated the more educated.[9]

The evidence that the Republican Party is losing some constituents is clear. Indeed in recent decades, perhaps the most visible sign of change for the party has been the steady erosion of its support within the Northeast. We will systematically examine change over time later in this volume, but a brief glimpse of the beginning

---

[5] For a review of this literature, see Hillygus and Shields, *The Persuadable Voter*, 1–48.

[6] V. O. Key, Jr., provided many insights in *Southern Politics in State and Nation* (New York: Knopf, 1949). Among the many excellent recent ones are: Thomas B. Edsall and Mary D. Edsall, *Chain Reaction: The Impact of Race, Rights, and Taxes on American Politics* (New York: W.W. Norton, 1991); Earl Black and Merle Black, *Politics and Society in the South* (Cambridge, MA: Harvard University Press, 1987); Earl Black and Merle Black, *The Vital South* (Cambridge, MA: Harvard University Press, 1992); and David Lublin, *The Republican South* (Princeton, NJ: Princeton University Press, 2004).

[7] Joshua Green, "The Rove Presidency," *Atlantic Monthly* (September, 2007).

[8] David Frum, "The Vanishing Republican Voter: Why Income Inequality is Destroying the G.O.P. Base," *The New York Times Magazine* (September 1, 2008), 48–51.

[9] Mark D. Brewer and Jeffrey M. Stonecash, *The Dynamics of American Political Parties* (New York: Cambridge University Press, 2009), 184–192.

and end of the time frame we examine indicates what has happened. In the congressional elections of 1894, New England elected twenty-six members of the House of Representatives. Twenty-five were Republican and one was a Democrat, John Francis Fitzgerald of Boston, known as "Honey Fitz." Fitzgerald, who would go on to be mayor of Boston, is best remembered as the grandfather of John, Robert, and Edward Kennedy. The near-complete Republican sweep of New England that year was almost matched by the party's showing in the rest of the Northeast. If we add to New England the states of Delaware, New Jersey, New York, and Pennsylvania, the Republicans carried 92 of the 100 seats in the Northeast.

One hundred and fourteen years later, the 2008 elections produced a unanimous House delegation from New England. This time, it was the Democrats who swept the region, winning all twenty-two seats. Christopher H. Shays of Connecticut was the one remaining Republican House Member following the 2006 elections, and he lost in 2008. In the Northeast as a whole, Democrats won sixty-eight out of eighty-four seats. Change was not confined to congressional elections. In the presidential elections of 1896 and 1900, Republican William McKinley won every northeastern state. In the presidential elections of 2004 and 2008, the Democratic presidential candidates won all the northeastern states. Over the course of a century, the Northeast has switched from heavily Republican to heavily Democratic.

The loss of the Northeast has cost the Republican Party. If the party had maintained a base in the region, it would have become the decisive majority party in the nation. Specifically, if the party had retained the Northeast:[10]

- George W. Bush would have won in 2000 with 360 electoral votes instead of 271. There would have been no Florida debacle, no *Bush vs. Gore* court controversy.

[10] The presidential election of 1948 and the congressional election of 1950 were relatively close, and we used those elections as a baseline for the "would haves" in the text.

- Bush would have won in 2004 with 374 electoral votes instead of 286. There would have been no controversy about voting in Ohio.
- Republicans would have controlled the Senate in the 110th Congress with a near-filibuster-proof 58 seats.
- Republicans would have ruled the House of Representatives in the 110th Congress with 229 seats.

In spite of the significance of the Northeast's counter-realignment, these changes have received little attention.[11] The South, which has made an equally dramatic shift and affected the direction of the nation as a whole, has received much more attention. This book is an attempt to correct that neglect and to consider the implications of this transformation for theories of party building. The essential issue is: What did the Republican Party do to lose its former electoral base? How have the strategy and actions of the party cost it voters in the Northeast? What did Democrats do to capitalize on Republican choices to try to win votes in the Northeast? The dynamic of the choices made by the two parties has transformed the Northeast, and our concern is why this has happened.

In pursuing an analysis of whom the party alienated in the Northeast, we could have just focused on the more general question of national changes. However, whereas national changes are clearly an important question,[12] a regional analysis is important for several reasons. First, regions may differ from other regions in the opinions that predominate. That was true of the South for decades, and as we shall show, it has also been true for the Northeast. That in turn affects the reaction within that region to national party positioning. Second, regions are more than collections of individuals. They encompass cultural patterns, past voting

---

[11] An exception is the examination of changes in the North. See Robert W. Speel, *Changing Patterns of Voting in the Northern United States* (University Park, PA: The Pennsylvania State University Press, 1998).

[12] For example, see Rebekah E. Liscio, Jeffrey M. Stonecash, and Mark D. Brewer, "Unintended Consequences: Republican Strategy and Winning and Losing Voters," in John C. Green, ed., *The State of the Parties* (New York: Rowman & Littlefield, forthcoming, 2010).

practices, likely prospects for winning states and districts, and possibilities for Electoral College votes, all of which affect political
calculations. Presidential candidates assess these aggregate level
conditions along with the views of voters in deciding whether to
pursue votes in a region. Finally, the Northeast is particularly interesting because for decades it was the base of the Republican Party,
its most reliable source of votes. What is most interesting is why
and how the party lost this base. The question is parallel to the
one concerning Democrats: Why did the Democratic Party pursue
liberals in the North and risk losing the South? Our concern is why
an area that provided Electoral College votes and congressional
seats for Republicans moved from one party to another.

THE NATURE OF CHANGE

The Northeast has swung from heavily Republican to heavily
Democratic. How do political changes of this magnitude occur?
Change did not happen abruptly but rather developed in stages.
Briefly from the 1890s until the 1930s, Republicans dominated
elections. Then the Great Depression resulted in voters in many
Northern cities shifting to the Democratic Party,[13] and from then
until the 1960s, Democrats were somewhat more competitive but
still the minority party in the Northeast. Starting in 1960, the
Northeast began to move decisively in the Democratic direction,
counteracting the movement of the South in the opposite direction. Then within the last decade, Republicans abruptly lost even
more ground in the Northeast.[14]

What creates these major shifts in partisan loyalties? That question has generated considerable debate. For some time, beginning
with studies in the 1950s, the presumption was that party attachments or identification were something acquired and essentially a

---

[13] James L. Sundquist, *Dynamics of the Party System: Alignment and Realignment of Political
Parties in the United States*, Revised Edition (Washington, DC: Brookings Institution
Press, 1983), chapters 8–10.

[14] David A. Hopkins, "The 2008 Election and the Political Geography of the New
Democratic Majority," *Polity* 41 (July 2009), 368–387.

"standing decision." That is, a stable identification with a particular party lasts for years until and unless something happens to make the voter reconsider which party is preferable. This argument dovetailed with that in the landmark study, *The American Voter*, which presented a portrait of a voter's "party identification" as one of the stable bedrock influences on how a person votes.[15]

If partisan loyalties are relatively firm, what explains the change within the Northeast? Change occurs in several ways. A significant social crisis, such as the Great Depression in the 1930s or civil rights battles in the 1960s, might prompt some voters to abruptly and permanently shift their partisan support.[16] Those same events might bring into the process many new voters who were previously unengaged.[17] They enter at a time when one party responds to their concerns, form an allegiance to that party, and remain attached to that party. Their entrance shifts the composition of the electorate and the fortunes of parties.

There might also be long, drawn-out processes that shift with party voters' support. The interests of groups change over time.[18] Voters are continually assessing the positions of the parties and deciding which to support.[19] As party positions shift, as expressed most prominently by presidential candidates, a voter decides to cast a ballot for the presidential candidate of a different party from the one the voter supported in the past. Over time, as the voter

[15] For early statements of this view, see V. O. Key, Jr. and Frank Munger, "Social Determinism and Electoral Decision," in Eugene Burdick and Arthur J. Brodbeck, eds., *American Voting Behavior* (Glencoe, IL: The Free Press, 1959), 286; and Angus Campbell, Philip E. Converse, Warren E. Miller, and Donald E. Stokes, *The American Voter* (New York: John Wiley and Sons, 1960). For a more recent statement, see Donald Green, Bradley Palmquist, and Eric Schickler, *Partisan Hearts and Minds: Political Parties and the Social Identities of Voters* (New Haven, CT: Yale University Press, 2002).

[16] For the 1930s, see the arguments of Sundquist, *Dynamics of the Party System.* For the 1960s, see Edward Carmines and James Stimson, *Issue Evolution* (Princeton, NJ: Princeton University Press, 1989).

[17] As an example, see Kristi Andersen, *Creation of the Democratic Majority* (Chicago: University of Chicago Press, 1979).

[18] David Karol, *Party Position Change in American Politics: Coalition Management* (New York: Cambridge University Press, 2010).

[19] Morris P. Fiorina, *Retrospective Voting in American National Elections* (New Haven, CT: Yale University Press, 1981).

casts more votes for the new party's presidential candidates, she begins to reconsider her votes for lower offices as well and gradually starts voting for other candidates of her new party. Finally, she comes to realize that she is more comfortable identifying with that new party, and the transformation is complete. Numerous studies of the political changes in the South over the past half-century suggest that those changes conform to this model, with changes beginning at the presidential level and working their way down to lower offices.[20] Southern whites, who had overwhelmingly identified with the Democratic Party since the Civil War, began voting for Republican presidential candidates in the 1950s. Eventually they started voting for Republicans for Congress and governorships, and later extended that behavior to local offices. Thus change can occur abruptly or gradually.

LEADING CHANGE: PRESIDENTIAL ELECTIONS

Much of the change that occurs in voting preference begins with presidential candidates. They are the most prominent party candidates and are the ones who can define a new direction for a party. The reasons they play this role will be developed in the next chapter. Figure 1.1 tracks the transition in results for that office. Until 1932, the Democratic share of the Northeast's presidential votes was usually well below 50 percent. The New Deal saw a dramatic rise in Democratic votes in the Northeast. That increase persisted, with some fluctuations, in subsequent decades.

Figure 1.1 also compares the Northeast with the rest of the country. From 1900 through 1924, the Northeast was less Democratic than the rest of the nation and always well below 50 percent. In six of the eight presidential elections from 1896 through 1924, the Republicans won every northeastern state. From 1932 through 1944, Democrats received more than 50 percent of the votes in the Northeast, but the region was still more Republican than the rest of the nation. From 1960 on, the Northeast became more

[20] Earl Black and Merle Black, *Politics and Society in the South* (Cambridge, MA: Harvard University Press, 1987), 259, 284–286.

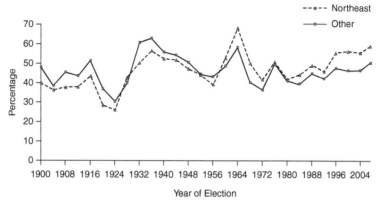

Figure 1.1. Democratic percentage of presidential vote, Northeast and remainder of nation, 1900–2008.

Democratic than the rest of the nation and stayed that way. Party decisions in those years and after are central to explaining why the Northeast has shifted to being so Democratic. In 1964, Lyndon Johnson became the first Democrat in history to carry every northeastern state, a feat duplicated twice by Bill Clinton in the 1990s, by John Kerry in 2004, and by Barack Obama in 2008.

THE HOUSE AND SENATE

If presidential candidates lead change, results for other offices should follow. All members of the U.S. House of Representatives are elected every two years, so this office is the most sensitive to change. Figure 1.2 shows some similarities and some differences to the patterns for presidential elections. As with presidential elections, Republicans did better in the Northeast than elsewhere in the first part of the twentieth century. The New Deal brought a major increase in Democratic success in the Northeast and elsewhere, peaking in 1936, and a subsequent decline by 1946. Democratic presidential candidates were able to make significant inroads into the Northeast, but Republicans in the House, after the losses of the early 1930s, were able to regain dominant majorities in the region from the late 1930s through 1960. While Democratic presidential

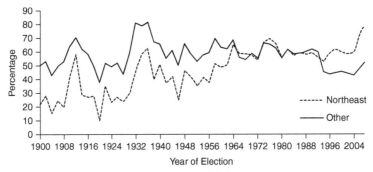

Figure 1.2. Democratic percentage of U.S. Representatives, Northeast and remainder of nation, 1900–2008.

candidates held consistent, if small, majorities or pluralities in the Northeast from 1960 on, House Democrats took longer to achieve that status. Democrats and Republicans divided seats within the region from 1960 through the mid-1990s, followed by significant Republican losses in the 2000s.[21]

Has the Senate followed the same path? Here our series begins in 1912, the first year when Senators were popularly elected. Since only one-third of the Senate is up for election every two years, changes in that institution are more likely to be gradual and take longer to occur than those in the House. Sure enough, Figure 1.3 shows slower rates of change than the previous two graphs did. There was the same New Deal bounce and post–New Deal fall in Democratic fortunes that occurred in presidential and House elections. Afterward there was essentially a gradual rise in Democratic support from the 1950s to the first decade of the twenty-first century, followed by an abrupt upward trend in 2006. It was not until 1980 that the proportion of Democratic Senators within the Northeast was greater than in the rest of the nation, followed by a pronounced increase in the 1990s. In comparison with elections for the president and House, Senate elections in the Northeast were not dominated by Democrats until later.

---

[21] For further documentation of these regional shifts, see Hopkins, "The 2008 Election and the Political Geography of the New Democratic Majority."

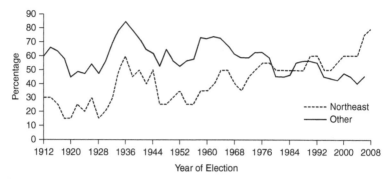

Figure 1.3. Democratic percentage of U.S. Senators, Northeast and remainder of nation, 1912–2008.

GUBERNATORIAL AND STATE LEGISLATIVE ELECTIONS

The patterns for gubernatorial and state legislative elections are different from what we have been observing. Figure 1.4 shows that the Democratic proportion of northeastern governors has fluctuated widely, especially in the first half of the twentieth century. To some extent, this fluctuation is due to the small number of governors in the Northeast – just ten. A partisan turnover of just a few governorships creates significant changes. Nevertheless, it is clear that starting in the late 1950s, Democrats were more consistently successful at electing governors in the Northeast than they had been in earlier decades. However, there was also a decline for twenty years after 1974, followed by a sharp rise. Democrats fared relatively poorly in electing governors in the Northeast until the 1950s and have roughly matched the national pattern since then. Why gubernatorial patterns differ from those of presidential and congressional elections is unclear, but it may be that elections for governor focus on state issues rather than national concerns, and are therefore affected by more random factors.

While changes for gubernatorial elections have been erratic, probably because of the small numbers, the changes in the partisanship of state legislatures have been fairly steady. Figures 1.5 and 1.6 indicate the average percentage of seats held by Democrats

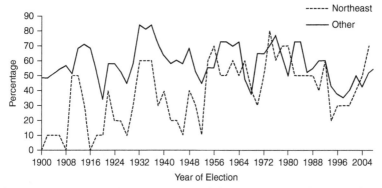

Figure 1.4. Democratic percentage of Governors, Northeast and remainder of the nation, 1900–2008.

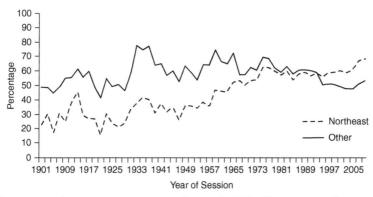

Figure 1.5. Average percentage of seats held by Democrats, State Houses, 1901–2009.

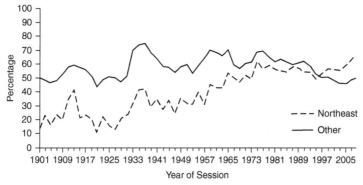

Figure 1.6. Average percentage of seats held by Democrats, State Senates, 1901–2009.

in state houses and senates since 1901.[22] As might be expected, following the top-down approach, the transition of the Northeast to Democratic dominance came later for these offices. It is not until the 1990s that in state legislative elections Democrats did better in the Northeast than elsewhere in the nation.

PARTY IDENTIFICATION

Finally, there is the matter of party identification. The American National Election Studies conducted by the University of Michigan ask people which party they identify with, and if they do not name one, which one they lean toward. Figure 1.7 shows the percentages choosing Democrats among those who identified with or leaned toward a major party.[23] It is a much smoother trend line than the others we have seen, a testimonial to how persistent people's partisanship is. In the Northeast, Democratic identification rose from the 1950s to the 1960s, gradually declined until 1984, and has risen since then. In comparison with the rest of the country, northeasterners were less Democratic in most years through 1984 and slightly more Democratic since then.

What sense can we make of all these trends? In comparing the Northeast to the rest of the nation, the process of regional changes in partisan voting largely follows the top-down pattern that prevailed in the South. This can be assessed in two ways: (1) when did the Democrats achieve at least 50 percent in a region and (2) when did they do relatively better in the Northeast than elsewhere in the nation? In presidential elections, Democratic candidates first reached 50 percent of the vote in the Northeast in 1932 but did not

[22] The information on partisan outcomes in state legislatures was compiled from various sources. For the years beginning in 1940, these results are available in the *Book of the States*. For recent years, the National Conference of State Legislatures (http://www.ncsl.org/programs/legismgt/elect/analysis.htm) provides results. For the years 1900–1938, the results are taken from Michael J. Dubin, *Party Affiliations in the State Legislatures: A Year by Year Summary, 1796–2006* (Jefferson, NC: McFarland and Company, 2007).

[23] Pure independents, or those who will not identify with either party, are excluded. The result is that the percentages are only of those with a preference as a denominator, so the reported percentages are higher than they would be if the base was all respondents.

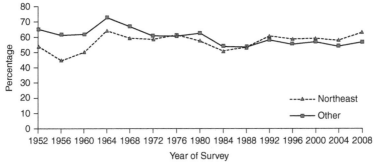

Figure 1.7. Democratic percentage of major-party identifiers and leaners, Northeast and remainder of nation, 1952–2008.

do relatively better in that region until 1960. House Democratic candidates gradually increased their percentage from 20 in 1900 to over 50 in 1934 and 1936 but they did not hit that level with any consistency until the 1960s. They first did relatively better in the Northeast in 1966 but did not consistently do better there until the 1990s. In the Senate, Democrats did not reach 50 percent until 1976 and did not do better within the Northeast until the early 1990s. In state legislatures, elected with the frequency of the House, Democrats were also able to reach 50 percent by the 1960s but they did not do relatively better in the Northeast until the 1990s. Presidential results led and others followed at a later date. The pattern for governors is simply more erratic.

PARTY DECISIONS AND THEIR EFFECTS: THE PLAN OF THIS BOOK

Our concern is the extent of partisan transition in the Northeast and why it has occurred. We will analyze the transition in some detail, with a focus on why Republicans lost the Northeast and what it tells us about the strategy of parties and the consequences of their strategy. These changes did not just happen but occurred because Republicans chose to pursue constituencies and policies that affected their ability to hold their former base.

We begin our analysis in the next chapter with a discussion of the logic of parties as they seek to maintain or create a majority.

We then use that framework to follow party decisions over time as they have sought to affect their fortunes and create a majority. Our approach is largely chronological as a way of tracking the major decisions parties have made over time and then assessing how these decisions affected the fortunes of the Republican Party within the Northeast. We argue that there have been three major junctures at which the Republican Party had to decide what direction their party would take. At each juncture, Republicans made strategic decisions that reduced their support in the region. We organize our analysis around those junctures.

Chapter 3 examines the first era of interest. From 1900 until 1930, Republicans dominated the Northeast. The party was then faced with how to respond to the Great Depression. Its response and the reaction of voters in the Northeast resulted in Democratic gains within the region during the 1930s. Those gains helped shift national party dominance to the Democrats from 1932 through the 1960s and presented Republicans, and particularly their presidential candidates, with the dilemma of how to create a majority. These choices are the focus of Chapters 4 and 5. The party decided to reaffirm its support for limited government, with minimal support for civil rights being one of their most prominent positions. This positioning, and the accompanying stance of Democrats, resulted in another sustained decline in Republican support in the Northeast. Chapter 6 then examines the development of the next and perhaps less clear-cut decision juncture the party faced. With the party acquiring more of a Southern base, it had to decide how much to respond to that growing party constituency and its more conservative concerns about social issues. Those decisions culminated in the further decline of the party in the Northeast in the elections of the 1990s and 2000s.

These changes have affected the success of Republicans within the region, and they have also affected the political voice emerging from the Northeast within Congress. That in turn has affected party polarization within Congress. Chapter 7 examines these changes. Finally, we return in Chapter 8 to the issue of how party decisions gain some constituents and cost the party others.

CHAPTER 2

Party Pursuits and the Sources of Change

Over the span of a century, the Northeast has gone from being solidly Republican to solidly Democratic. What explains such a dramatic transition? How does a party lose a region that from 1870 to 1930 was solidly Republican and from 1932 to 1964 was at least divided between the two parties? The answer involves the nature, purposes, and pursuits of parties.

American political parties are loose coalitions of elected officials, activists, and groups with diverse interests. Those who work within a party may be motivated by the desire to win power, to enact specific policies, or both. They presumably have some commonality of concerns, which may involve ideology, regional history, economics, cultural concerns, ethnicity, group identity, or some combination of these and other factors. Although those working within a party may share some common purposes and the desire to win the next election, the party rarely acts as a unified, unitary actor. The "party" is often composed of actors with differing views of what policy positions the party should be pursuing and what strategies will bring victory.[1] Elites seek to shape these internal

---

[1] In adopting this view we are following a long line of theorists who see parties as coalitions composed of groups that often disagree on specific policies. Those conflicts lead to arguments about future directions. They create situations in which elites must maneuver among competing policy concerns. See for example E. E. Schattschneider, *Party Government* (Westport, CT: Greenwood Press, 1942), 64; V. O. Key, *Parties, Politics, and Pressure Groups*, 5th ed. (New York: Thomas Y. Crowell, 1965), 344; and Howard L. Reiter, "Factional Persistence within Parties in the United States," *Party Politics*, Vol. X,

debates but just as often end up reacting to and trying to cope
with competing policy demands. The initiatives for policies come
as much from groups wanting some policy as from elites seeking
to win the votes of groups. Sometimes greater unity is created by
tamping down differing demands: Leaders argue that only if unity
occurs will wins be achieved, which then may provide the opportunity to enact desired policies. Other times, divisions erupt and
create significant internal conflict. The process of elite, group,
and activist interactions is ongoing.

The dynamics of these interactions may also vary considerably
by "wing" of the national party. The congressional wing may have
a clear base and wish to maintain and respond to it. A presidential candidate may see potential votes among other groups and
pursue voters that will clash with the existing congressional base.
Competing groups may well create significant policy conflicts for
which political elites must negotiate some resolution. Out of all
these interactions emerge a party image and a set of policy concerns that may vary in clarity from time to time.[2]

These interactions are not static. Some components of a party
may be content with the current electoral base and policies, and
others may wish to change the direction of the party to pursue
new voters and policies. There are debates about the efficacy of
responding to certain groups. Will a new direction hurt or help
the party? Will it bring new voters? There are continual efforts to
assess how voters react to expressions of concern about issues and
policy enactments. These discussions about change are particularly important when a party is in the minority. In that case, party
members regularly propose strategies to pull voters away from
the other party. The process of pursuing new constituents may be

No. 3 (May 2004), 251–271. Each emphasizes the enduring role of groups within parties. For an excellent overview of the group-based view and the transition to the view
of parties as elite-dominated unitary actors (the Downsian view), see Marty Cohen,
David Karol, Hans Noel, and John Zaller, *The Party Decides: Presidential Nominations
Before and After Reform* (Chicago: University of Chicago Press, 2008), 20–40.

[2]   See Richard J. Trilling, *Party Image and Electoral Behavior* (New York: Wiley, 1976); and
Mark D. Brewer, *Party Images in the American Electorate* (New York: Taylor and Francis,
2008).

lengthy and gradual: The party seeks to pry older voters away from their prior loyalties and also to convince younger and newer voters that they should consider identifying with their party.

This process of parties' efforts to expand or alter their electoral base is the source of electoral change.[3] Changes do not just happen to parties; they are not helpless victims of social and economic vicissitudes. Sometimes events or trends present parties with the need to react. A Great Depression occurs, marchers increase the pressure for civil rights laws, or social conservatives become increasingly distressed about perceived social decay or rising abortion rates. Groups within the party make arguments about how the party should respond to political and economic developments, and the decisions made eventually generate positive reactions among some groups and negative reactions among others. Other times, parties actively formulate plans about how to pull voters away from the opposing party.

Regardless of what prompts party decisions, the positions adopted affect the party image presented to voters. Voters gradually perceive these images and decide which party they wish to support. In a process we call secular realignment, voting groups gradually shift their allegiance from one party to the other[4] as they perceive shifting party concerns and images.[5] These efforts of parties may not always lead to the results hoped for or expected. Parties sometimes simply misjudge the likely effects of their actions, as when Republicans in 1964 nominated Barry Goldwater, who lost disastrously. By the late 1990s, Republicans had become

[3] Alan Ware, *The Democratic Party Heads North, 1877–1962* (New York: Cambridge, 2006), 16; Kenneth Feingold and Theda Skocpol, *State and Party in America's New Deal* (Madison, WI: University of Wisconsin Press, 1995), 51.

[4] The initial statement of this was V.O. Key, Jr., "Secular Realignment and the Party System," *Journal of Politics* 21 (1959), 198–210. For an excellent example of applying this to change within the South, see Earl Black and Merle Black, *Politics and Society in the South* (Cambridge, MA: Harvard University Press, 1987).

[5] As stated by Morris Fiorina, *Retrospective Voting in American National Elections* (New Haven, CT: Yale University Press, 1981), voters form "running tallies" of the parties and gradually change. For additional and more recent evidence, see Jeffrey M. Stonecash, *Political Parties Matter: Realignment and the Return of Partisanship* (Boulder, CO: Lynne-Rienner, 2006), 109–128.

more responsive to social conservatives, which brought them votes
in the South but cost them votes elsewhere.

There may also be abrupt changes in political fortunes that surprise everyone. Republicans, benefiting greatly in 1994 from a
general negative reaction to the Democratic Party, took over the
Senate and the House of Representatives. However, though short-
term changes occur unexpectedly, the more important sources of
long-term change involve the decision making and planning of
parties.

In making the argument that party planning leads to gradual
change, we set aside as less useful another common explanation
of change – critical realignment.[6] That framework presumes that
changes in partisan loyalties happen in relatively abrupt bursts.
Parties at some point in time have an accumulated electoral base,
and their leaders have adopted a set of policy positions to respond
to that base. Social and economic changes then occur, but leaders do not perceive these changes or are unwilling to respond.
Perhaps they do not recognize public frustrations or are afraid to
respond to new problems with different policies because doing so
would antagonize their existing electoral base. Frustrations build
over time, and eventually social change and events push new issues
on the agenda. Some voters abruptly shift their allegiances out of
frustration about a lack of response from the party in power, which
creates new electoral alignments. Central to this explanation of
change is the notion that political leaders either cannot discern
shifting concerns or for some reason do not respond. In the critical
realignment framework, incremental change is unlikely because
leaders do not adjust to changing social conditions.

The enduring example of an abrupt change occurring was
during the Great Depression. Republican Herbert Hoover was the
president as the Great Depression began with the stock market

---

[6] The most widely cited argument for this is Walter Dean Burnham, *Critical Elections
   and the Mainsprings of American Politics* (New York: W.W. Norton, 1970). The idea
   was originally presented by V. O. Key, Jr., "A Theory of Critical Elections," *Journal
   of Politics* 17 (1955), 3–18. It has also been restated recently by Arthur C. Paulson,
   Electoral Realignment and the Outlook for American Democracy (Boston: Northeastern
   University Press, 2007).

crash in 1929, creating a negative image for Republicans and eventually resulting in the nation becoming more Democratic. Some might interpret this change as one in which party leaders do not create changes in electoral alignments, but find change largely occurring to them. This partisan shift, however, was not inevitable. It was a result of party choices. Hoover was committed to limited government and did not advocate policy proposals sufficient to revive the declining economy. The 1932 election then produced a significant increase in support for the Democratic Party.[7] Franklin Roosevelt knew the election results were largely a rejection of Herbert Hoover and the Republicans. He recognized that he had acquired an electoral base that he would have to work at retaining with a legislative program.[8] Change was sustained because of the positions of party leaders.

We argue that parties are entities continually assessing the political environment and calculating how they can expand their electoral base. They struggle with balancing existing commitments to principle and the desire to attract new constituents. As they seek new constituencies, they also worry about whom they might lose as they shift emphases.[9] Party leaders are entrepreneurs seeking to shape their future and are not merely blown around by forces beyond their control. Parties make policy choices and those choices have been central in the changes we will examine.

PRESIDENTIAL POLITICS AND THE ELECTORAL COLLEGE

Although we often speak abstractly of parties as unified actors seeking to advance policies, they are in reality a collection of

7 James L. Sundquist, *Dynamics of the Party System: Alignment and Realignment of Political Parties in the United States*, Revised Edition (Washington, DC: Brookings Institution Press, 1983).
8 Lizabeth Cohen, *Making a New Deal: Industrial Workers in Chicago, 1919–1939* (New York: Cambridge University Press, 1990); and David Plotke, *Building a Democratic Political Order: Reshaping American Liberalism in the 1930s and 1940s* (New York: Cambridge University Press, 1996).
9 Kevin P. Phillips, *The Emerging Republican Majority* (New York: Anchor Books, 1970), 464–465.

candidates largely conducting independent campaigns. In particular, congressional and presidential wings of the party differ in the role they play in creating change. Congressional party candidates must respond to their state and local constituencies to get elected. If the constituencies of congressional members are diverse, congressional candidates will resist announcing a uniform party position as they focus on local adaptation and survival. As a collection of elected officials, they often express differing positions, which casts doubt on the idea of a unified national party. When party organizations recruit new candidates, they recognize the importance of respecting diverse situations and generally seek to support party candidates who may win, regardless of their ideological conformity to some desired party position. They may prefer candidates ideologically compatible with the party, but any elected party member is better than one from the other party.

This recognition and accommodation of diversity have implications for the focus and concerns of congressional parties. They desire a majority to pursue principles and policies, and they may have a strategy to gradually expand their electoral base, but they also know they will have to work with the existing diversity of states and districts. As a result, it has generally been unusual for a congressional party to present a unified national image to the electorate.[10] It can happen, but the tug between working with current members and trying to expand makes clarity of image difficult. Furthermore, it is not always necessary for a congressional party to achieve a majority to have some policy impact. Even in a bad year, a party usually retains a significant number of seats in the House and Senate. As a minority, the party has multiple mechanisms to affect the political and legislative process. A majority may be desired but it is not a necessary condition to having an effect.

Presidential campaigns differ from those of congressional candidates in two ways that are important for creating partisan change. First, presidential candidates must pursue a strategy that creates a

---

[10] As will be discussed later, the 1994 election was an unusual situation in that the House congressional party did take a position and it had a positive effect.

majority of Electoral College votes. Presidential candidates must try to combine policy principles with the pragmatic need to secure enough electoral votes to win the Electoral College.[11] A presidential campaign plan cannot settle for relying on the existing base if that base does not constitute a majority. The majority sought is not just a majority of the popular vote, but a majority of the Electoral College. Presidential candidates who come from a party that is currently in the minority must seek a coalition of state victories that is broader than the party's existing base. Candidates in this situation have a strong imperative to be agents of change. A congressional party can plan and hope for an expanded base and pursue that with great focus, but as noted earlier, the party does not have to have a majority to have some policy impact. Presidential candidates, however, must always focus on garnering a majority.

The second difference is that presidential candidates have a relatively high influence on party image. They articulate a relatively uniform national message that is covered nationally by the mass media. They receive greater media coverage, get more voter attention, and have a greater effect on how voters see a party. Presidential campaigns are times when there is more message dissemination and greater voter attention, thus presidential positions can define the apparent concerns and positions of parties. Congressional parties, on the other hand, contribute to a party image by the policy votes and legislative enactments they engage in prior to an election. Both the congressional and presidential wings of parties matter in creating change, but presidential candidates are more likely to seek a national majority and are more likely to express and obtain coverage for a uniform message. This creates a situation in which presidential candidates have greater potential to be agents of partisan change. Sometimes that outcome is negative,

---

[11] For the significance of the Electoral College see Scott C. James, *Presidents, Parties, and the State: A Party System Perspective on Democratic Regulatory Choice, 1884–1936* (New York: Cambridge University Press, 2000). For evidence on these matters see Jeffrey M. Stonecash, "The Electoral College and Democratic Responsiveness," in Gary Baugh, ed., *Electoral College: Challenges and Possibilities,* (Aldershot, UK: Ashgate, 2010), 65–76.

as it was for Republican presidential candidates such as Hoover in 1932 and Goldwater in 1964. Sometimes the effect is positive, as with Ronald Reagan in 1980 and 1984.

THE DILEMMAS OF PURSUING A MAJORITY

Republican presidential candidates, facing minority status, have been the primary source of changes in the Northeast. Table 2.1 indicates the situation that Republican presidential candidates have faced. From 1900 to 1928, Republican candidates won six of eight elections and on average won 60.7 percent of the Electoral College votes. Their base was the Northeast and all seemed well. Then from 1932 to 1964, the party lost seven of nine elections. Those losses and their situation in Congress prompted the Republican candidacies of Barry Goldwater (1964), Richard Nixon (1960, 1968, and 1972), and Ronald Reagan (1980 and 1984) to seek a different electoral base. They felt that their party had to pursue votes in the South, and that pursuit led to much greater overall success in the years 1968–2004. That decision and the subsequent policy appeals lead to one of the central concerns of this analysis: the potential negative effects of pursuing new constituents. For every constituency pursued with expressions of sympathy for their interests, there is the risk of losing another. Republican decisions have attracted some and alienated others.

To pursue new constituents, a party needs a relatively clear identity and a message that appeals to the new, targeted constituents. That message can be expressed by both presidential and congressional candidates. The central issue is the extent of difference between the views of current and targeted constituents. The greater the policy differences between existing and targeted constituents, the greater the risk of alienating the current constituents with the new message.[12] If the positions that appeal to the newly targeted groups alienate the existing base, the problem for

---

[12] D. Sunshine Hillygus and Todd G. Shields, *The Persuadable Voter: Wedge Issues in Presidential Campaigns* (Princeton, NJ: Princeton University Press, 2008), 45.

TABLE 2.1. *Party success in presidential elections by years, 1900–2004*

Years	Party and campaigns won	Democratic % of		Republican % of	
		Popular vote	Electoral College	Popular vote	Electoral College
1900–1928	R – 6 / 8	40.1	39.3	50.2	60.7
1932–1964	D – 7 / 9	52.6	66.0	45.8	34.0
1968–2004	R – 7/10	44.9	36.5	49.3	63.5

the party is whether to continue with the changed emphasis. Is the party winning enough votes and seats with the new constituency to make up for the support lost, such that the change is worth pursuing?

The issue of whether pursuing different positions might lose existing constituents also depends on what the opposing party decides to do. Is the opposing party taking action to exploit the developing tensions in its opponent's own ranks?[13] Leaders of the opposing party might also increase their efforts to hold on to the constituency they have currently, or they might decide that they do not mind losing that constituency if they think they can gain enough newer constituents.

THE DISJOINTED PROCESS OF CHANGE

As a party contemplates whether it should pursue change and considers the possible consequences, assessment is not simple. A presidential candidate may pursue a changed image and succeed with no negative effects. The average party vote among the current constituency may decline only slightly because party congressional incumbents are well known and have large campaign finance war chests. The party may retain its seats within a region that was its traditional base, but with lower levels of electoral support. The power of incumbency in House and Senate elections may conceal

---

[13] Paul Frymer, *Uneasy Alliances: Race and Party Competition in America* (Princeton, NJ: Princeton University Press, 1999).

the costs of a new party position until several years later. Thus the effects of new party positions on partisan support within the existing constituency will lag. Furthermore, in the Senate, with only one-third of members up for election every two years, the effects may be delayed even longer. In the short term, the party may be able to continue with a coalition of the existing and newer constituencies, and not have to contend with the full effects of the changing strategy of the party.

It is also true that many voters pay little attention to politics, and some may only gradually perceive that the policies pursued by the party are shifting. Thus, as transitions occur, the party image may not be as consistent as it once was. However, some voters recognize change while others do not. The party may still win votes among its traditional constituents because many supporters may not see the extent to which the party is shifting its emphasis. It also means there is a time lag in how quickly many voters perceive change and alter their party identification. The result is that there is not clear and rapid feedback to the party of the consequences of its shifting concerns.

Eventually, as the composition of the party changes with relatively more members coming from the new constituency, and its new policy positions are repeated and its image becomes more unified, more voters will recognize the policy shifts. As incumbents who represent the current constituency retire, they might be replaced by members from the other party. Again, whether that happens depends on the actions of the other party. But as newer themes are pursued, the image and constituency of the party gradually change.

The recognition of party change by voters may also take longer if the party has not yet acquired a majority. As the minority party, its policy proposals are likely to receive less prominence. Once the party becomes the majority and enacts its policy agenda, to the extent that its policies clash with its traditional constituency, even more voters will see the difference and defect to the other party.

PARTY DECISIONS AND CHANGE IN THE NORTHEAST: AN OVERVIEW

The dynamics just reviewed have played out in the Northeast and changed the overall partisan dispositions of the region. For Republicans, there have been three crucial junctures at which they have had to decide what direction the party would take. The first involved the issue of what stance to take regarding the New Deal (the 1930s). The second involved a decision about how to expand their appeal into the South and escape being largely a minority party (the 1960s). The third involved the extent to which the party would respond to its growing support among social conservatives (the 1980s–2000s).

Each had significant consequences for the party within the Northeast. Subsequent chapters will develop how these changes occurred in some detail. At this point we wish to provide a brief overview of the choices each party faced, how the decisions changed party bases, and the consequences for partisanship in the Northeast.

Republican Dominance and Confronting Crisis: 1900–1930s

Following the 1896 election, the Northeast became more Republican.[14] For the first three decades of the 1900s, Republicans were the majority party in the Northeast. That base, plus their substantial success in the remainder of the nation, generally gave them a national majority. The elections of the late 1800s and early 1900s had witnessed fundamental arguments about capitalism, labor, and the role of government. Republicans did well in those

---

[14] Just how much the region moved Republican in 1896 is a matter of dispute. Walter Dean Burnham argues that there was a significant realignment in 1896 that created large Republican majorities [Walter Dean Burnham, *Critical Elections and the Mainsprings of American Politics* (New York: W.W. Nortn, 1970)]. There are others who argue that the evidence suggests a much more modest increase. See David R. Mayhew, *Electoral Realignments: A Critique of an American Genre* (New Haven, CT: Yale University Press, 2002); Alan Ware, *The Democratic Party Moves North;* Jeffrey M. Stonecash and Everita Silina, "Reassessing the 1896 Realignment," *American Politics Research*, 33, no. 1 (January, 2005), 3–32.

elections, and during the early 1900s, the party generally saw the political support they received as an endorsement of their positions of promoting capitalism and individualism while generally limiting the role of government.[15]

Democrats were usually in the minority, with most of their electoral base coming from the South. In the North they fared relatively better in many larger cities than in rural and small town areas,[16] but the party did not win enough congressional seats in the North to be able to expand its national electoral base. The Northeast was a particularly difficult region for Democrats: Neither the presidential nor congressional wing of the party could consistently win substantial segments of the Northeast. Democrats realized that they had to make inroads into the Northeast, or it would be difficult for them to win the presidency and achieve a majority in Congress. The difficulty for the party was that its Southern wing was rural and uneasy about urban life, Catholics, and immigrants.[17] Indeed, many members of the congressional party were hostile to Catholics, supported prohibition, and wanted to restrain immigration.

The dilemma for Democrats was that the Northeast was steadily becoming more urban, immigrants were becoming a larger portion of the population, and more of them were achieving citizenship and the right to vote. The problem was whether the Southern wing of the party could overcome its antipathy to Northern urban life and immigrants in order to create a majority. The result was a lengthy battle between the rural and urban wings of the party over the presidency and the policies that should be pursued. To reach out to urban immigrant populations would alienate the Southern

[15] See John Gerring, *Party Ideologies in America, 1828–1996* (New York: Cambridge University Press, 1998).

[16] Samuel J. Eldersveld, "The Influence of Metropolitan Party Pluralities in Presidential Elections since 1920: A Study of Twelve Key Cities," *American Political Science Review* 43 (December, 1949), 1189–1206; Samuel Lubell, *The Future of American Politics*, 2nd ed., Revised (Garden City, NY: Doubleday Anchor Books, 1956); Carl N. Degler, "American Political Parties and the Rise of the City: An Interpretation," *Journal of American History* 51 (June 1964), 41–59.

[17] David Burner, *The Politics of Provincialism: The Democratic Party in Transition 1918–1932* (New York: Knopf, 1968).

rural areas, as occurred in the 1928 election when Irish Catholic Governor Al Smith of New York was the party's presidential candidate. There was considerable conflict in the party about whether to pursue this expanded base.

The Great Depression, at least for a while, resolved the Democrats' dilemma. Republicans, faced with a dramatic economic collapse, chose to oppose significant government intrusion into capitalism and fight against government assistance for individuals. The electorate rejected the Republican position, and Democrats won substantial votes in the North in the 1930s, giving them control of the presidency and the Congress.[18] For the next several decades, the additional base the Democrats had acquired in the Northeast was enough to give them a relatively sustained national majority. The saving grace for Republicans was that the Democratic Party was limited by internal divisions. The voters Democrats added in the northern urban areas were ethnics (Irish, Italians, Poles) and blacks, and minorities. And Southern Democrats were not receptive to either.

As the Democratic star rose nationally and in the Northeast, Republican fortunes waned. The dilemma for the Republicans was how to respond to Democratic New Deal programs, which were popular around the country, but especially in the Northeast. Through 1936, although a vocal progressive wing of the Republican Party backed much of the New Deal, the party's leaders mostly opposed those programs, resulting in continuing losses, especially in the Northeast. Only late in the decade did northeastern Republicans begin to moderate their position and start to win elections again.

The 1960s, the Role of Government, and Party Choices

The 1960s presented each party with fundamental choices. For Democrats the question was how much to respond to Northern urban interests and how to interpret subsequent election results as a

[18] Kristi Andersen, *The Creation of a Democratic Majority 1928–1936* (Chicago: University of Chicago Press, 1979); Julius Turner and Edward V. Schneier, *Party and Constituency: Pressures on Congress*, Revised Edition (Baltimore: Johns Hopkins Press, 1970).

guide to what policy directions they should pursue. For Republicans the issue was how to react to Democratic policy enactments and how to expand their electoral base to escape being a minority.

The Democrats' success in the 1930s gave them a base in the North, but it was not a stable base. In the 1940s and 1950s, the party struggled to maintain and build its support within that region.[19] The question of whether and how to expand the party's base into the North emerged again in 1960 and 1964. Democratic presidential candidates realized that their margins in these states were small, and they needed to take steps to increase their support in the North.[20] They also realized that seeking this expansion could hurt their support within the South. Responding to minority concerns about civil rights issues such as the right to vote, access to housing, desegregation, expanded rights to welfare, and expansion of other programs might alienate the South. The election results of 1958–64 appeared to resolve the issue in favor of a liberal agenda, and the party acted on the concerns of the newer, more liberal constituents. The result was the remarkable outpouring of legislation constituting the Great Society and a significant expansion of the role of the federal government.

While Democrats were struggling with the problem of expanding their base, Republicans were simultaneously engaged in a debate about whether to fundamentally change direction.[21] Following the 1930s, Republicans were largely a minority party. A much higher percentage of voters identified with the Democratic Party both in and outside the South. By 1968, Democrats had held the presidency for twenty-eight of the previous thirty-six

---

[19] Philip Klinkner, *The Losing Parties: Out-Party National Committees 1956–1993* (New Haven, CT: Yale University Press, 1995), 12–40.

[20] For Kennedy's situation, see Frances Fox Piven and Richard A. Cloward, "The Politics of the Great Society," in Sidney M. Milkis and Jerome M. Mileur, eds., *The Great Society and the High Tide of Liberalism* (Amherst, MA: University of Massachusetts Press, 2006), 257; for Johnson's, see Sidney M. Milkis, "Lyndon Johnson, the Great Society, and the Modern Presidency," in Milkis and Mileur, eds., *The Great Society and the High Tide of Liberalism*, 1–49.

[21] This battle is reviewed in Nicol Rae, *The Decline and Fall of Liberal Republicans from 1952 to the Present* (New York: Oxford University Press, 1989).

years, and they had controlled Congress most of those years. Two groups within the Republican Party presented contending arguments about what direction the party should take. The pragmatists thought the country was moderate and more accepting of a greater role for government. They thought the party had to accept some safety-net national programs such as Social Security while still promoting business and individualism. New York Governor Nelson Rockefeller embodied much of this view. In contrast, the principled conservatives thought the party had mistakenly capitulated to the New Deal notion that government should play a greater role, and that the party had abdicated its role as a party of opposition.[22] They were convinced that the party had to stand for conservative principles, and many felt that these principles would appeal to Southerners.[23] The outburst of liberal legislation that Democrats began to enact in 1964 further convinced conservatives that the party had to take a different path. The candidacy of Barry Goldwater was a product of this concern.[24] The shift in emphasis was also evident in the party's change from supporting civil rights laws to arguing that government had gone too far in such legislation.[25]

The 1968 candidacy of Richard Nixon was also an important juncture for the party.[26] Nixon was somewhat of a conservative, but by 1968 he was primarily focused on putting together a coalition that would win. After losing the 1960 presidential contest and the 1962 California gubernatorial election, he was determined not to

---

[22] Donald T. Critchlow, *The Conservative Ascendancy* (Cambridge, MA: Harvard University Press, 2007); Niels Bjerre-Poulsen, *Right Face: Organizing the American Conservative Movement, 1945–1965* (Copenhagen: Museum Tusulanum Press, 2002); John Micklethwait and Adrian Wooldridge, *The Right Nation: Conservative Power in America* (New York: Penguin Press, 2004).

[23] William Rusher, "Crossroads for the GOP," *National Review*, February 12, 1963, 109–112; the argument about how the party could expand its base was made in Phillips, *The Emerging Republican Majority*. See also Klinkner, *The Losing Parties*.

[24] Richard Perlstein, *Before the Storm* (New York: Hill and Wang, 2001).

[25] Edward G. Carmines and James A. Stimson, *Issue Evolution: Race and the Transformation of American Politics* (Princeton, NJ: Princeton University Press, 1989).

[26] Richard Perlstein, *Nixonland: The Rise of a President and the Fracturing of America* (New York: Scribner, 2007).

lose again. He had watched George Wallace transform populism from government protecting "little people" from large corporations to protecting "the people" from government telling them how to live and with whom to associate. Nixon, seeing Wallace attract votes using this theme, eyed the South as a region where he could win votes.[27] He also knew that he had to be careful not to sound too much like Wallace because he could alienate Northern, more moderate Republican voters. Nixon indicated that he would be restrained in pursuing desegregation and busing as he sought to appeal to a new Southern constituency while not alienating the more moderate constituency of the North.

This second major decision juncture embodied the dilemma of a minority party. It had to decide if its efforts to expand into the South would help it win votes and whether such efforts might cost it support in the North. The positions of Goldwater and Nixon, and the shifts in party positions in Congress on issues such as civil rights, moved the party to the right. The party gained in the South but its support within the Northeast declined.

Republicans and Social Conservatives

Despite doing fairly well in presidential elections after 1968, Republicans remained largely in the minority in Congress. They gained a majority in the Senate for six years in the 1980s, but had been in the minority in the House since 1954. The party was steadily pursuing and winning seats in the South, and the 1994 election finally brought Republicans a majority in both houses of Congress. The question was how to interpret the election and govern with this new power.[28] The leadership of the party was now dominated by Southerners, and the party was facing pressures to pursue the policies of cultural conservatives – but the Northeast wing was not receptive to this emphasis. The party again had to decide what direction it would pursue and what costs it might

[27] Dan Carter, *The Politics of Rage: George Wallace, the Origins of the New Conservatism, and the Transformation of American Politics* (New York: Simon and Schuster, 1995).

[28] Daniel J. Balz and Ronald Brownstein, *Storming the Gates: Protest Politics and the Republican Revival* (Boston: Little, Brown, and Company, 1996).

incur if it responded to the pressures of cultural conservatives. The party chose to devote more attention to the concerns of social conservatives. As it did so, the support of the party within the Northeast declined even further.

THE EFFECTS OF DECISIONS

Party decisions matter for those the party attracts and those it loses. In the 1930s, the Republican response to the economic crisis was widely seen as inadequate, and the party lost many Northern urban voters. In contrast, Democrats were seeking a broader Northern base, and the Great Depression gave them an opportunity to build support within that region. Those inroads, unsteady as they were, provided the basis for the party to pursue greater support there in the late 1950s and 1960s. The decisions of the 1960s again hurt Republicans in the Northeast. While Democrats were becoming more liberal in the 1950s and 1960s, Republicans were moving in a conservative direction. The combination of Democrats advocating liberal positions and Republicans becoming more conservative in the 1960s pushed the more moderate Northeast into greater support for the Democratic Party. Later, as the Republican Party acquired power in 1994 and pursued a clear and more visible socially conservative agenda, the contrast between the parties became even clearer, and the Northeast became even more Democratic.

In retrospect, the logic of change seems clear. The process by which decisions were made and partisan change unfolded, however, was erratic. The implications of decisions were not always evident to the actors involved. The story of the decisions made, their consequences, and how transition occurred are our next concerns.

CHAPTER 3

The First Republican Losses

Democratic Gains in the 1930s

OVERVIEW

From 1900 through 1926, Republicans dominated the Northeast. Democrats did somewhat better in 1928 in the region, and then from 1930 to 1936 they made major gains. While Democrats lost some of those gains by 1940, Republican support never returned to the level that prevailed in 1900–26. The Democratic gains of the 1930s were echoed in the rest of the nation and made the Democrats the national majority party for decades to come.

Why did this first transition occur? Much of the change is attributed to the Great Depression. Republicans were in power when it began in 1929 and in response the electorate blamed them and voted Democratic. However, this was not a simple case of economic events determining change. The transformation in the Northeast was also a product of party strategies. Parties make choices and create identities and that affects whom they attract or lose. The Northeast had undergone significant social change, becoming more urban and populated by immigrants. The Democratic Party, with some internal conflict, was trying to respond to these social trends and make inroads into the region. They had a long-term goal of bringing industrial workers, city dwellers, and immigrants and their descendants into the party. The Great Depression finally brought them those groups, but then Roosevelt had to work to retain them. The party enjoyed some modest gains among these groups even in the 1920s, but not to the level that occurred in the

1930s. Economic events may have precipitated partisan change, but it was political decisions that solidified those changes.

The more fateful decisions were those made by Republicans. They first provided a very limited response as the Great Depression developed. They then decided to oppose Roosevelt's New Deal as its social and economic thrust became clear. Voters in the Northeast became among the New Deal's strongest supporters, and this resulted in a crushing defeat for the Republicans in the off-year gubernatorial and congressional elections of 1934 and in Roosevelt's re-election in 1936. For decades, northeastern Republicans had stood out as the most conservative wing of the party. Those decisions cost them in the Northeast.

The Republican Party was not, however, incapable of interpreting and reacting to election results. Recognizing and accepting what had occurred may have taken a while, but the party did adjust. Late in the 1930s, northeastern Republicans were able to stave off further erosion by moving to the center and accepting some of Roosevelt's programs. That transition probably prevented further decline.

REPUBLICAN DOMINANCE

The 1890s marked a watershed in politics for the Northeast and for the nation as a whole. A severe depression in the early part of the decade led to the public's repudiation of Democratic president Grover Cleveland, resulting in a massive shift of voters toward the Republicans in the congressional elections of 1894 – the elections that left Honey Fitz Fitzgerald as the only Democratic Representative from all of New England. Then in the presidential election of 1896, Nebraska Democrat William Jennings Bryan squared off against Ohio Republican William McKinley. Bryan was a fiery orator who spoke for rural America. He castigated the corporate elite of his day and was anathema in the urban and industrial parts of the country, foremost of which was the Northeast. Bryan created an image of a party not sympathetic to urban life, immigrants, and industrialization. The result was that voters in the Northeast became uneasy with the Democratic Party, and McKinley became the first presidential candidate in twenty-four years to carry every northeastern state. That feat was duplicated by McKinley in 1900 when again his opponent was Bryan, and by fellow Republicans Theodore Roosevelt in 1904 and William Howard Taft in 1908. Republicans had defended industrial capitalism and its provision of jobs. They were clearly the party of industrialism, hard money, and the protective tariff, and were rewarded for these stances by dominating elections in the Northeast.[1] The result is evident in House elections. Republicans moved from winning fewer than 50 percent of seats in the Northeast in the early 1890s to consistently winning 70 percent or more. As Figure 3.1 indicates, they occasionally won more than 50 percent of House seats elsewhere in the country, but the most solid base of the party was the Northeast. From 1894 through 1926, Republicans generally won at least 70 percent of House seats within the Northeast.

The only real exception to this dominance occurred in 1912. A deep split occurred within the Republican Party in that year, which led to the third-party Progressive candidacy of Theodore Roosevelt. Teddy Roosevelt recruited many candidates to run on his party line, drawing what might have been Republican votes to Progressive candidates. The result was a division of likely Republican votes between Republican and Progressive candidates, which enabled Democrat Woodrow Wilson to sweep most of the Northeast. Four years later, however, the Republicans reunited, and Wilson won only one northeastern state, New Hampshire, while eking out a narrow victory in the nation as a whole. Soon the pre-1912 pattern re-emerged, and Republicans swept every northeastern state in 1920 and 1924, and all but two in 1928.

---

[1] Just how quickly this shift occurred, whether abruptly in 1896 or gradually after 1896, is in dispute. For analyses suggesting the change was abrupt, see Walter Dean Burnham, *Critical Elections and the Mainsprings of American Politics* (New York: W.W. Norton, 1970); and James L. Sundquist, *Dynamics of the Party System*, Revised Edition; for more skeptical treatments, see David R. Mayhew, *Electoral Realignments: A Critique of an American Genre* (New Haven, CT: Yale University Press, 2002); and Jeffrey M. Stonecash and Everita Silina, "The 1896 Realignment: A Reassessment," *American Politics Research* 33 (January 2005): 3–32.

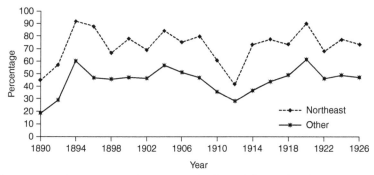

Figure 3.1. Percentage of seats won by Republicans in the House of Representatives, Northeast and elsewhere, 1890–1926.

Following the 1928 elections, it would be hard for Republicans not to have seen America as receptive to its message of limited government. The party continued to be supportive of industrial capitalism and industrialization, and accepted urbanization as a natural part of a more industrial society. The party usually won all the Electoral College votes in the Northeast and dominated House and Senate elections. Herbert Hoover won the presidency in 1928, completing three consecutive presidential elections won by Republicans since 1920. From 1900 through 1928, Republicans won six of eight presidential elections and did so by dominating the Northeast. Of the elections within the Northeast during 1900–28, Republicans won an average of 73.1 percent of all House seats. After popular elections of U.S. Senators began in 1912, Republicans won 81.5 percent through 1928. In state legislatures in the Northeast, the party won an average of 70.5 percent of all seats in state houses and 76.1 percent of all seats in state senates. The Republicans' national situation seemed secure in large part because of their success in the Northeast.

SOCIAL CHANGE

While Republicans were well established in the Northeast, it was a region undergoing change. As Figure 3.2 indicates,[2] more and

[2] The data are from the *U.S. Statistical Abstract.*

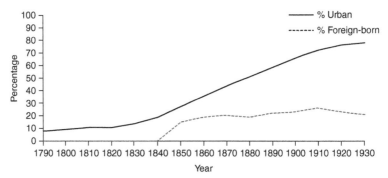

Figure 3.2. Changes in the Northeast: urbanization and immigration.

more people were moving to urban areas and by 1930, 78 percent of the population lived in an urban area. Immigration was steadily occurring, with most of that population settling in urban areas. More and more of this urban population – natives and immigrants – worked in factories.

The Northeast was Republican but it was increasingly not a region of just rural or native-born Americans. It was a region that Democrats had sometimes sought to appeal to by sponsoring legislation to regulate working conditions and restrain large corporations.[3] The party, however, faced three fundamental problems in securing the votes of urban workers. First, most did not see politics, much less the national government, as relevant to their lives. Many came from a culture that emphasized self-reliance and support from their extended family if help was necessary. Government was not seen as a solution to problems.[4] Second, as a result, most were not registered to vote and as a consequence were of little political relevance.[5]

Finally, even if urban residents had been motivated to focus on politics, they would have had a hard time seeing the Democratic

[3] Elizabeth Sanders, *Roots of Reform: Farmers, Workers, and the American State, 1877–1917* (Chicago: University of Chicago Press, 1999), 340–408.
[4] Lizabeth Cohen, *Making a New Deal: Industrial Workers in Chicago, 1919–1939* (New York: Cambridge University Press, 1990).
[5] Kristi Andersen, *The Creation of a Democratic Majority 1928–1936* (Chicago: University of Chicago Press, 1979).

Party as receptive to them.[6] The Democratic Party derived its primary base from the Protestant rural South, which was not receptive to immigrants, Catholics, and urban life. Southern votes had played a major role in enacting prohibition in 1919 and the limits on immigration that were established in the early 1920s. For example, seven southern and three border states were among the first fifteen to ratify the Prohibition (Eighteenth) Amendment in 1918, and no southern votes were cast in either house of Congress against the restrictive Immigration Act of 1924. Also in 1924, the party held its national convention in New York City and, after a prolonged and public battle, narrowly defeated a motion condemning the Ku Klux Klan and took 103 ballots to deny New York Governor Al Smith the presidential nomination. In the late 1920s, it would have been hard for an urban immigrant to see the Democratic Party as clearly more sympathetic to his or her concerns.

In contrast, Republicans had consistently argued that the private sector should be left alone because it brought jobs. They argued that its support for the protective tariff on imported goods protected urban jobs. Enough workers had responded to this message that Republicans had become "the party of the rising cities."[7] The comparison of the two party images hindered the appeal of the Democratic Party. "The nativism of Southern and Western Democrats along with the pro-business stance of Republicans made it hard for urban working-class and lower middle-class groups to find a place in either party."[8]

The result was that Democrats did not receive strong support in urban areas. In large cities, the Democratic vote for House candidates fluctuated around 50 percent from 1900 through 1924, with

[6] David Burner, *The Politics of Provincialism: The Democratic Party in Transition 1918–1932* (New York: Alfred A. Knopf, 1968).

[7] Carl N. Degler, "American Political Parties and the Rise of the Cities: An Interpretation," *Journal of American History* 51 (June 1964), 48. See also Burner, *The Politics of Provincialism*, 18.

[8] David Plotke, *Building a Democratic Political Order: Reshaping American Liberalism in the 1930s and 1940s* (New York: Cambridge University Press, 1996), 82–83.

no trend evident.[9] In those same cities, Democratic presidential candidates generally received less support because they lacked the local roots and attention to urban concerns of House candidates. Outside urban areas in the Northeast, the party continued to struggle to attract much support.

CRISIS AND CHANGE

After years of Democratic frustration, the 1928 elections carried the seeds of future Democratic gains. The Democratic big-city presidential vote was unusually low in 1920 and 1924 but rebounded handsomely in 1928.[10] The party's presidential nominee that year was Governor Alfred E. Smith of New York, the first Roman Catholic nominee of a major party. He was an outspoken exemplar of the immigrant ethnic culture from which he had sprung, and his opposition to the prohibition of alcohol seemed to fit right in with that stance. While Smith lost many votes elsewhere in the nation because of his religion, he carried normally Republican Massachusetts and Rhode Island and managed to run better in the popular vote in the Northeast than in the rest of the country, the first time a Democrat had done so. The Democratic efforts to create some support among big-city ethnic groups were beginning to pay off. While Smith lost his bid for the White House, his candidacy suggested the potential for Democratic gains in Northern urban areas.

As often happens in politics, the party was then helped by unforeseen events and the response of Republicans. In October 1929, the stock market plummeted and the Great Depression began to unfold. Employment and incomes declined steadily. Republican President Herbert Hoover, supported by the private sector, believed in the virtues of coordinated efforts among business to maintain prices

[9] Alan Ware, *The Democratic Party Heads North, 1877–1962* (New York: Cambridge University Press, 2006), 156–157; and Burner, *Politics of Provincialism*, 21.
[10] Burner, *Politics of Provincialism*, 20. See also Degler, "American Political Parties," 52–56; and Andersen, *The Creation of a Democratic Majority 1928–1936*, 28.

and production. He was opposed to any efforts to have the federal government play any significant role by establishing government programs or spending money. He was also continually advised by economists and advocates for business that the economy would be self-correcting and that government intrusion would only slow the adjustment process. If left alone, private actors would adjust their prices and wages and demand would revive.[11]

By November 1930, the economy did not improve and the electorate held the Republican Party accountable. In the congressional elections that fall, Republicans lost fifty-one seats in the House and eight in the Senate. Despite this setback, the Republican Party remained committed to limited programs and minimal intervention in the economy. The unemployment programs that existed were limited and run by the states,[12] and the party was opposed to establishing a national program to help those unemployed. With conditions worsening by late 1932, Franklin Roosevelt, the Democratic nominee for president, knew that Hoover would be held accountable for the economic problems. He decided not to present any detailed plans for helping the economy, and count on a negative electoral reaction to Republicans. Democrats swept to power in 1932, gaining another 100 seats in the House and 12 in the Senate.

Roosevelt was now President and had to decide what to do about the Depression. Both his congressional party and Republicans had to decide how to react to any proposals he presented. The magnitude of the Great Depression and the acquisition of power presented a possibility for Democrats. Roosevelt could not be certain how his congressional party would react, because some Democrats, especially in the South, adhered to the Jeffersonian belief that the best government is that which governs least.[13] Along with

[11] Arthur Schlesinger, Jr., *The Age of Roosevelt* (Boston: Houghton Mifflin, 1957); Sundquist, *Dynamics of the Party System*, Revised Edition, 199–204; and Anthony J. Badger, *The New Deal: The Depression Years* (Chicago: Ivan R. Dee, 1989), 41–54.

[12] Edwin Amenta, *Bold Relief: Institutional Politics and the Origins of Modern American Social Policy* (Princeton, NJ: Princeton University Press, 1998), 3–79.

[13] Sundquist, *Dynamics of the Party System*; and Badger, *The New Deal: The Depression Years*, 54–57.

Republicans, they opposed proposals for new federal programs in the late 1920s.

The political situation was changing, however. For most of the years since 1900, a majority – sometimes larger, sometimes smaller – of House Democrats came from the South. The new entrants in the House in 1930 and 1932 relegated the South to a lower percentage of the party. After the 1932 elections, Southern Democrats were only 32 percent of the congressional party, whereas northeasterners comprised 18 percent, and members from other areas totaled 50 percent. The newer members were more inclined to support action by the federal government. Furthermore, the newer members from the North now had more of an urban base, and Democrats wanted to build on their success in these districts. Roosevelt's success was another sign of change. He was the first Democratic president in history who could have won his first two terms without any southern Electoral College votes.

From the middle 1920s to the early 1930s, there was a significant expansion of the electorate with most of it coming in large urban areas and almost all of it was voting Democratic.[14] Urban immigrants who had long been used to self-reliance, family support, or help from ethnic organizations were now seeing government assistance as relevant to their lives, and were registering and voting.[15] The addition of these new voters in urban areas provided a base for significant gains for the Democratic Party in the 1930s. Figures 3.3 and 3.4 indicate just how great the gains were and where they were. As Figure 3.3 indicates, in Northeast House elections prior to 1928, Democrats were unable to get above an average of 40 percent of the vote even in districts with the greatest density.[16] Their percentage in such districts was about the same

---

[14] Andersen, *The Creation of a Democratic Majority 1928–1936.*
[15] Cohen, *Making a New Deal: Industrial Workers in Chicago, 1919–1939.*
[16] These districts are grouped as follows: 0–59 population per square mile are in the least dense category. Those with 60–999 are in the middle category, and those with 1,000 or more per square mile are in the most dense or most urban category. For a discussion of the creation of this data set, see Jeffrey M. Stonecash, *Parties Matter: Realignment and the Return of Partisan Behavior* (Boulder, CO: Lynne Rienner, 2006), 137–143.

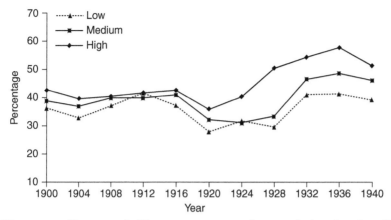

Figure 3.3. Democratic House percentages by population density of districts, Northeast, 1900–40.

as in the more rural districts. Then in 1928, the party was able to win an average of 50 percent of the House vote in the more urban districts, and they won 30 of the 73 districts (41 percent) in this group. The 1932 elections further increased their success in the most urban districts, to 55 percent of the vote in those districts. The party made gains in the districts with less population density in 1928 and 1932, but their average and percentage of seats won remained below 50 percent in those districts. The party now had a significant base in the Northeast.

The change was even more pronounced in presidential elections, as shown in Figure 3.4. Democratic presidential candidates had not done well in urban areas in 1920 and 1924 because the party nominated presidential candidates with little urban appeal. Smith's candidacy marked an abrupt rise in the Democratic presidential vote in the more urban districts. In 1932, the party did even better in these districts.[17] The nomination of Smith followed by the Great Depression had dramatically improved the party's

[17] Carl Degler, "American Political Parties and the Rise of the Cities: An Interpretation," *Journal of American History* 51 (June 1964), 41–59; and Samuel J. Eldersveld, "The Influence of Metropolitan Party Pluralities in Presidential Elections since 1920: A Study of Twelve Key Cities," *American Political Science Review* 43 (December 1949), 1189–1206.

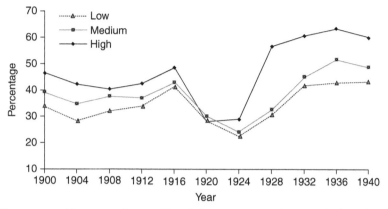

Figure 3.4. Democratic presidential percentages by population density of House districts, Northeast, 1900–40.

fortunes in the more urban districts. The party's gains in these districts were distinctly greater than in the less urban districts.

THE NORTHEAST AND THE NEW DEAL

With the Great Depression at its zenith in 1932, the nation overwhelmingly elected Franklin Delano Roosevelt president. In that election, however, the Northeast still remained as the most Republican section of the nation. All six states that Roosevelt failed to carry were in that section. As Figure 3.5 shows, the increase in the Democratic vote from 1928 to 1932, or for that matter from 1920 to 1932, was lower in the Northeast than it was in other parts of the nation. Despite his being governor of New York, northeastern voters were more resistant to Roosevelt's appeal than the rest of the electorate. Democrats had improved their fortunes in the Northeast, but Republicans still were dominant.

It is important to understand what happened and what did not happen in 1932. That election was largely a repudiation of the past four years of Herbert Hoover's Republican administration and its failure to bring the nation out of the Depression. In every state, the Democrats improved their showing over that of 1928; the mean presidential Democratic gain was nearly 20 percent. Because

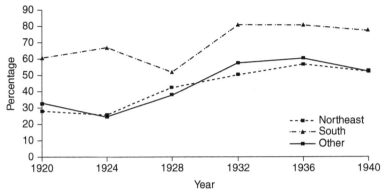

Figure 3.5. Democratic percentage of presidential vote, by section, 1920–40.

of Roosevelt's often ambiguous campaign pledges, and because so much of his program became apparent only after he took office, the vote in 1932 could not be taken as a guide to what people might think of the New Deal. His challenge was to take actions that would retain the votes he had received in 1932. Only later elections, which would be in large part a verdict on Roosevelt's program, would provide such a guide.

In the first couple of years, the New Deal consisted largely of programs to deal with the economic crisis and treat all classes similarly. For example, its landmark program, the National Recovery Administration (NRA), organized collaborations among business, labor, and the public to set "codes of competition" for many industries. As time went by and more radical proposals were put forth by other public figures, Roosevelt began to move to the left and adopted programs that included Social Security, an unemployment compensation program, the minimum wage, and protection of labor unions' right to organize. These and other programs had strong appeal in the big cities of the Northeast, where so many residents were in need of financial aid, where public works projects transformed the face of urban America, and where rising labor unions organized industrial workers and benefited from New Deal labor programs. In the words of Arthur Schlesinger, Jr., "The urban masses became the central preoccupation of the

Second New Deal."[18] The result was the sustained high Democratic vote that we saw in Figures 3.3 and 3.4.[19] In subsequent elections, Democrats received higher votes in urban areas and among ethnic immigrants and blacks.[20]

REPUBLICAN PARTY CHOICES

Electoral movements are not responses to the policies of just one party. As Roosevelt presented legislation and his New Deal program came into focus, the Republican Party had to make another choice, that of how much to oppose Roosevelt and how much to go along with him. From a fairly early date, but especially after Roosevelt's move to the left, most Republicans decided to oppose the New Deal.[21] In retrospect, we may well wonder why they chose to work against one of the most popular presidents in history. In the context of the times, however, the Republicans had every reason to hope that Roosevelt's victory in 1932 was a fluke, a short-term response to the economic calamity, and that the Republicans would soon be restored to their majority status. They had held power for several decades, they believed, and were likely to return to that status.

No Republican was more fervent in advocating a hard line against the New Deal than former President Herbert Hoover, who only two months after Roosevelt took office, wrote to Ohio Senator Simeon Fess to argue:

[18] Arthur M. Schlesinger, Jr., *The Politics of Upheaval* (Boston: Houghton Mifflin, 1960), 423.

[19] Ware, *The Democratic Party Heads North*, 164, 173.

[20] M. Stephen Weatherford, "After the Critical Election: Presidential Leadership, Competition and the Consolidation of the New Deal Realignment," *British Journal of Political Science*, 32, no. 2 (April, 2002), 221–257; and Rita Werner Gordon, "The Change in the Political Alignment of Chicago's Negroes During the New Deal," *The Journal of American History*, 56, no. 3 (December, 1969), 584–603; Andersen, *The Creation of a Democratic Majority*.

[21] On the Republicans in the 1930s, see Clyde P. Weed, *The Nemesis of Reform: The Republican Party During the New Deal* (New York: Columbia University Press, 1994); and Thomas M. Slopnick, *In the Shadow of Herbert Hoover: The Republican Party and the Politics of Defeat, 1932–1936*, doctoral dissertation in History, the University of Connecticut, 2006.

..... that the GOP could not survive if it attempted to follow those leaders who sought to "compete in demagoguery and socialism" with the Democrats, nor could it survive if it followed other leaders who sought to compromise with the New Deal. He continued to believe that the Republican party could attract a majority if it continued to be a "defender of constitutional methods ..." If the GOP failed to demonstrate its fidelity to these principles it would be "the end of this civilization." Eventually, Hoover said, more of the people would "return to the principles I have stated – and two million more of them [supporters] in the last election would have given a majority."[22]

Hoover did not believe that the voters, faced with the choice between a moderate Republican "partial New Dealer" and a Democratic "100 percent New Dealer," would choose the former. He predicted that if the Republicans did not wholeheartedly oppose the New Deal, they would die as the Whigs had in the nineteenth century. By sticking to principles, the party would hold on to its core constituency and attract Jeffersonian Democrats. [23]

The northeastern wing of the party became the primary source of opposition. This faction had long been the home of the most conservative Republicans, as shown in Figure 3.6. The figure shows the average ideological scores that have been computed by Keith Poole and Howard Rosenthal, which measure a dimension "that represents conflict over the role of government in the economy," the central issue of the New Deal.[24] The higher the score the more conservative the voting records of members. Until the late 1930s, northeastern Republicans in both houses of Congress were considerably more conservative than their counterparts outside the region.

This general conservatism within the Northeast translated into greater opposition to the New Deal, as indicated in an

[22] Gary Dean Best, *Herbert Hoover: The Postpresidential Years 1933–1964: Volume 1: 1933–1945* (Stanford, CA: The Hoover Institution Press, 1983), 8–9; the author's brackets.
[23] Ibid., 19, 30; and Slopnick, *In the Shadow of Herbert Hoover*, 298.
[24] Keith T. Poole and Howard Rosenthal, *Congress: A Political-Economic History of Roll Call Voting* (New York: Oxford University Press, 1997), 35.

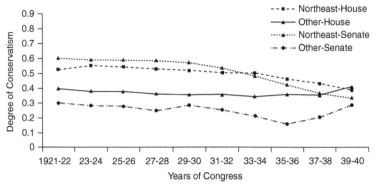

Figure 3.6. Degree of conservatism of Republican members of Congress, by section, 1921–40.

analysis by Clyde Weed. He calculated the percentage of times each Republican who served in Congress between 1933 and 1938 voted for key New Deal proposals.[25] As Figure 3.7 shows, northeastern Republicans in both houses of Congress were considerably less likely than other Republicans to support the New Deal.[26]

A party can never know in advance how its positions will be received by the electorate. While northeastern Republicans thought that their region would swing back to supporting them, they had to wait until the off-year congressional elections of 1934 to receive voter reactions to their opposition to the New Deal. The 1934 elections were the first off-year elections in decades in which the president's party increased its number of seats in Congress. Perhaps most important was that, as shown by Figure 3.8, the increase in Democratic seats from 1932 to 1934 in the House of Representatives was confined to the Northeast. In the rest of the country, Democratic success either leveled off or declined. Outside the Northeast, the big gain in Democratic seats occurred between 1930 and 1932. In the Northeast, it happened *after* Roosevelt's first two years. Clearly the New Deal was striking a responsive chord in Roosevelt's home region. The Republican Party's opposition to the New Deal was not helping it in the Northeast.

[25] Weed, *Nemesis of Reform*, 213–219.
[26] *Ibid.*, 13, 120, 145–148.

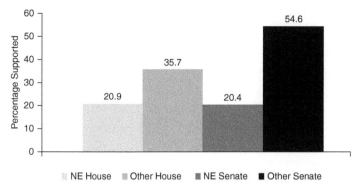

Figure 3.7. Percentage of votes on major New Deal legislation on which Republicans in Congress supported the New Deal, by House and section, 1933–38.

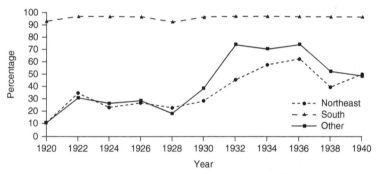

Figure 3.8. Democratic percentage of seats in the House of Representatives, by section, 1920–40.

There were other indications of Republican weakness in the Northeast in 1934. A poll by the *Literary Digest* found the greatest gains in Roosevelt's popularity "centered in such previously Republican strongholds as Pennsylvania, Connecticut and New York." Four conservative Senators from the Northeast lost their re-election bids in 1934.[27]

Some northeastern Republicans saw the writing on the wall and tried to moderate their party's stand as early as 1934, but with

[27] Weed, *Nemesis of Reform,* 44, 55.

limited success. The old Teddy Roosevelt ally Gifford Pinchot ran as a supporter of the New Deal in Pennsylvania's Republican Senate primary, but lost. The chairman of the New York State Republican Party was ousted after he came out against attacking the New Deal. On the other hand, a Republican Senator from Rhode Island spoke out against criticizing Roosevelt, and in Pennsylvania, local Republican organizations endorsed five Democratic Representatives running for re-election. Even a veteran conservative, former national chairman Charles Hilles of New York, could see the writing on the wall. The day before the election, he wrote, "[We] little dreamed in June that the public would be as apathetic and unsympathetic as it is today. We felt it here in the summer and realized that it was more pronounced in the east than in the west."[28]

Despite the 1928, 1930, 1932, and 1934 election returns, many Republicans remained optimistic that the 1934 election results were again a fluke, attributable to the votes of people on relief. The northeastern Republicans were apparently politicians of principle who had faith in the durable appeal of their ideals. They thought that old strategies would work in the upcoming presidential election of 1936. In 1935, a conference of New England Republicans in Boston endorsed a conservative stance, and the party made gains in local elections in the Northeast later that year. Republican opposition to the New Deal in Congress increased, with eastern Representatives voting 94 percent against Roosevelt's program, and Senators voting 90 percent against it.[29]

Republican hopes were quickly dashed when the pattern of 1934 recurred when Roosevelt ran for re-election in 1936. In the presidential election (Figure 3.5) he made his greatest gains from 1932 in the Northeast. His vote in the Northeast in 1936 was 6.3 percent higher than it had been in 1932, compared with a drop of 0.3 percent in the South and a gain of only 2.6 percent in the rest of the country. In the House the party also made its greatest gains

[28] Weed, *Nemesis of Reform*, 37–40; and Slopnick, *In the Shadow of Herbert Hoover*, 236.
[29] Weed, *Nemesis of Reform*, 69, 86, 92–93, 165.

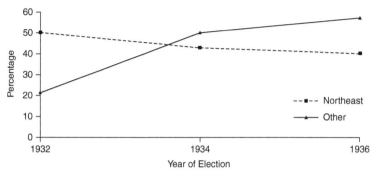

Figure 3.9. Percentage of Republican-held Senate seats retained by the party, by section, 1932–36.

from 1932 in the Northeast. The same pattern prevailed in the Senate. Figure 3.9 shows the fate of Republican-held Senate seats in the elections of 1932, 1934, and 1936. Through the course of Roosevelt's first term, Republicans were increasingly likely to hold onto their Senate seats outside the Northeast, but decreasingly likely to hold them in the Northeast. Northeast Republicans had opposed the New Deal and the feedback was becoming clear: their opposition was costing them seats and elections.

In the aftermath of the 1936 debacle, some prominent northeastern Republicans began to reassess their strategy. Archconservative Representative Hamilton Fish of New York told his party's state committee,

> For sixteen years the party that we belong to has invariably fought Franklin D. Roosevelt and Governor [Herbert] Lehman, and the result has been that we have not elected a Governor in sixteen years.... I want to keep the door open and not shut it to the wage earners and the liberals.

And Governor Harold Hoffman of New Jersey said, "The Republican Party is hampered by leaders who are still living among cobwebs and mothballs."[30]

---

[30] Quotations from Henry Fairlie, *The Parties: Republicans and Democrats in This Century* (New York: Pocket Books, 1978), 36–37.

MORE PARTY DECISIONS AND THEIR EFFECTS

In the 1938 and 1940 presidential and congressional elections, Republican fortunes in the Northeast improved substantially. Two matters were important in this change. First, Roosevelt's second term turned out to be politically more challenging than his first. His attempts to increase the size of the Supreme Court in 1937, to defeat conservative Democrats in the 1938 primaries, and to assume substantial powers to reorganize the federal government all failed, partly due to an emerging alliance between Republicans and conservative Democrats concentrated in the South.[31] Roosevelt had overreached and his pursuit of power harmed his image. In the 1938 elections, Republicans made substantial gains in all parts of the nation outside the South.

The Republican Party also began to change as it underwent a transition in its composition. Many of those ousted in the 1930s were among the most conservative. Their departure gave the party fewer conservative voices to represent its positions. Northeastern Republicans also finally realized that archconservatism was a serious liability. There was an increase in moderate Republicans who were downplaying the party's opposition to the New Deal and emphasizing what the chair of the New York State party called "a humane program of its own." Such appeals marked gubernatorial campaigns in Connecticut, Massachusetts, New York, and Rhode Island, and Senate races in New Jersey and Pennsylvania. Newly elected governors of New Hampshire and Vermont urged the Republican National Committee to take a more moderate public stance.[32] As indicated in Figure 3.6, the voting record of northeastern Republicans in Congress became less conservative and that of western Republicans moved to the right. By the 1940s, the lines had crossed, and ever since, northeastern Republicans have anchored their party's liberal wing. By and large, the process

---

[31] James T. Patterson, *Congressional Conservatism and the New Deal: The Growth of the Conservative Coalition in Congress, 1933–1939* (Lexington, KY: University of Kentucky Press, 1967).

[32] Weed, *Nemesis of Reform*, 195–197.

by which this transformation occurred was the replacement of departing members by Republicans more in tune with their section's ideology: moderates in the Northeast and conservatives elsewhere. The combination of Roosevelt's overreaching and the change in the ideological composition of the Northeastern delegation of the Republican congressional party stopped the loss of Republican seats in the region.

PARTY STRATEGIES IN THE 1930s

Perhaps the most striking feature of party strategies in the early 1930s is how little they had changed from prior decades. What changed were the results that followed from the strategies. At least since the realignment of the 1890s, many northern Democrats had sought to capture the urban vote by appealing to the urban, labor, and ethnic electorate. These efforts culminated in Al Smith's unsuccessful presidential candidacy in 1928. Roosevelt's victory four years later was based on a continuation of that strategy, along with appeals to the South and West with promises of aid to agriculture and the development of public power. These policy stances attracted many traditionally Republican progressives to the Democratic coalition. His policies to help the unemployed brought him the votes of urban workers and their families as the 1930s progressed. As for the Republicans, the opposition to federal government activism that had crystallized in the 1920s carried over to the New Deal, when most of the party opposed much of Roosevelt's program.[33] In short, neither party departed from prior strategic initiatives in the 1930s.

What did change in the 1930s was the economic, social, and political environment in which the parties were operating. Crushed by economic hardship, the public was increasingly receptive to using

[33] On developing party ideologies, see John Gerring, *Party Ideologies in America, 1828–1996* (Cambridge, England: Cambridge University Press, 1998). On Roosevelt's wooing of Republican progressives, see Scott C. James, *Presidents, Parties, and the State: A Party System Perspective on Democratic Regulatory Choice, 1884–1936* (New York: Cambridge University Press, 2000), 200–266.

government at all levels to repair the economy and provide social services for vulnerable people. This development had different effects on the two major parties. The Democrats were in the right place at the right time, with the right programmatic approach. An experimenter by temperament, Roosevelt was willing to try whatever means would pull the nation out of the Depression and provide some degree of security for the people. In an often-quoted speech in May 1932, he advocated "bold, persistent experimentation. It is common sense to take a method and try it; if it fails, admit it frankly and try another. But above all, try something."[34] Roosevelt was not a blank slate, however; he was a product of the progressive movement of the early twentieth century and an admirer of his relative, Theodore Roosevelt, who had been a proponent of a more vigorous federal government. Much of Franklin Roosevelt's agenda was drawn from that of progressivism, and the public approved. On the other hand, Republican opposition to most of the New Deal facilitated Democratic efforts to portray that party as heartless, stuck in outmoded ways of thinking, and ineffectual at solving the nation's problems – images that kept the Republicans in minority status for decades.

These policy stances of Republicans hurt them in the Northeast, where the electorate was notably approving of the New Deal as it evolved in the mid-1930s. In 1929, for example, Republicans controlled nine out of ten of the Northeast's governorships, seventeen out of twenty of its Senators, and 76 percent of its Representatives in Congress. Eight years later, the GOP claimed only 40 percent of governors and Senators and 37 percent of Representatives. Increasingly, northeastern Republicans made their peace with the New Deal and shifted toward the center of the ideological spectrum, thereby paving the way for a revival of their fortunes in the 1940s and 1950s. This shift created a split within the national party, as Republicans elsewhere in the nation were less disposed to moderate their stance. Thomas E. Dewey, who ran a strong race for

---

[34] Speech at Oglethorpe University in Atlanta, May 22, 1932; quoted in R. G. Tugwell, *The Brains Trust* (New York: Viking Press, 1968), 105.

governor of New York in 1938, won that office four years later and
led his party's moderate wing and won its presidential nomination
twice in the 1940s, articulated his pragmatic approach in 1950:

> These impractical theorists with a "passion for neatness" … would
> have everything very neatly arranged, indeed. The Democratic
> Party would be the liberal-to-radical party. The Republican
> Party would be the conservative-to-reactionary party. The results
> would be neatly arranged, too. The Republicans would lose every
> election and the Democrats would win every election.[35]

Dewey's approach would characterize northeastern Repub-
licanism for at least a generation. Fellow governors like Nelson
A. Rockefeller of New York (whose grandfather and namesake,
Nelson Aldrich, had been a very conservative Senator from
Rhode Island) and William W. Scranton of Pennsylvania, and
Senators like Margaret Chase Smith (Maine), George D. Aiken
(Vermont), Edward W. Brooke (Massachusetts), Lowell P. Weicker,
Jr. (Connecticut), Jacob K. Javits (New York), Clifford P. Case
(New Jersey), and Hugh Scott (Pennsylvania) would lead the
party's liberal wing for many years. That faction would also domi-
nate national party conventions from 1940 to 1960, nominating
Republican liberals like Wendell L. Willkie (1940), Dewey (1944
and 1948), and Dwight D. Eisenhower (1952 and 1956), and moderate Richard M. Nixon on a liberal platform heavily influenced
by Rockefeller in 1960.

Party conflicts over what direction to take, however, were not
over. While northeastern Republicans became a moderating
influence within the party, the conservative wing was not ready
to accept this adjustment. As Senator Robert A. Taft of Ohio, the
leader of the party's conservative Old Guard, said in 1952: "A party
kills itself and removes any excuse for its existence when it adopts
the principles of its opponents."[36] This debate about the proper

[35] John A. Wells, ed., *Thomas E. Dewey on the Two-Party System* (Garden City, NY: Doubleday & Co., Inc., 1966), 9.
[36] Quoted in Russell Kirk and James McClellan, *The Political Principles of Robert A. Taft* (New York: Fleet Press Corp., 1967), 52.

stance for the GOP in a liberal era would continue into the 1960s, the next time that changes in the electoral environment provided opportunities for parties to change their strategies and woo new blocs of voters – with further profound consequences for politics in the Northeast.

CHAPTER 4

Searching for a Majority, the Rise
of Conservatives, and Second Losses

OVERVIEW

Beginning with the elections of 1932, Democrats won six of the next eight presidential elections. From 1932 through 1962, Democrats held the majority in the House and for fourteen of sixteen elections they held the Senate. The Republican losses in the 1930s and 1940s created the disagreements within the Republican Party that were discussed in the preceding chapter. Persistent losses also presented the party with the need to reassess their situation in the Northeast. Three issues were important. First, the party had experienced a decline not only outside the Northeast, but also within its northeastern historical base. This diminished support in their historical base suggested that the party had significant problems. Second, even if the party was able to rebuild its strength in the Northeast, the region was slowly declining as a percentage of the nation's population and as a percentage of Republican votes. It was providing fewer Electoral College votes and House seats. Rebuilding support within the region might not pay off enough to make it worthwhile. Third, a conflict was developing about the value of continuing to regard the Northeast, with its relatively more moderate delegation in Congress, as the base of the party. The northeastern wing of the party had been its most conservative up until the 1930s and the staunch core of the party. As noted earlier, Members of Congress from this region began to move to a more moderate position in the 1930s. This movement created consternation among the more conservative members of the party and set the stage for a battle between the liberal-moderate and conservative wings of the party, a battle the outcome of which eventually had serious effects on the party's fortunes in the Northeast.

THE DECLINE IN REPUBLICAN SUPPORT WITHIN THE NORTHEAST

The formation of the New Deal coalition diminished the fortunes of northeastern Republicans in presidential and House elections. As Table 4.1 indicates, in the presidential elections from 1900 through 1928, Republicans averaged 59.6 percent of the vote in northeastern states. With Electoral College votes allocated on a winner-take-all basis, and with Republicans winning almost all the Northeast states, that enabled the party to win an average of 97.1 percent of states and almost all Electoral College votes. This gave the party a solid basis for winning presidential contests. In House elections for 1900 through 1928, northeastern Republican candidates averaged 56.5 percent of the vote. Their margin in House elections in the region was not impressive, given the party's dominance of the region, but the margins were enough to allow them to win an average of 80.3 percent of seats for that period. Outside the Northeast, the party was only able to win about 50 percent of the vote in presidential or House elections, but they won in enough states and districts to generally achieve a national majority.[1] The Northeast plus enough of the remainder of the country generally kept the party in power for three decades.

The 1932 elections reduced Republican support in the Northeast, and the party could not regain it in subsequent years. In presidential elections, the party did well only in 1952 and 1956, but support again declined in 1960. Only in 1956 did the party

---

[1] While the Republican Party was able to maintain a majority for most of the years 1900–28, their average margin of victory across the nation was still less than that enjoyed by Democrats. See Jeffrey M. Stonecash, *Reassessing the Incumbency Effect* (New York: Cambridge University Press, 2009), 93.

TABLE 4.1. *Republican Presidential and House electoral fortunes, 1900–28 and 1932–60, national and by section*

	Average 1900–1928	Average 1932–1960	Change
Presidential			
Average State Percentage of Vote			
Nation	49.5	44.4	−5.1
Northeast[2]	59.6	51.1	−8.5
Remainder	46.7	42.7	−4.0
Percentage of States Won			
Nation	67.7	39.7	−28.0
Northeast[3]	97.1	63.8	−33.3
Remainder	59.9	36.0	−23.9
House			
Average District Percentage of Vote			
Nation	46.9	39.3	−7.6
Northeast[4]	56.5	48.1	−8.4
Remainder	43.1	36.0	−7.1
Percentage of Districts Won			
Nation	59.7	38.5	−21.2
Northeast	80.3	54.3	−26.0
Remainder	51.6	34.4	−17.2

surpass its 1900–28 average, and the average percentage of the presidential vote won during 1932–60 dropped to 51.1 from the previous average of 59.6. In House elections, the yearly average of

[2] These are the averages within each era of yearly averages. That is, the average within a year is first calculated and then those averages are averaged for the years 1900–28. This focus on averages, and not the percentage of the vote won within the entire region, is because the Electoral College requires winning within a state, so the percentage won within a state is important. All averages for 1900–28 exclude 1912. For the Northeast, with 1912 included, the average is 55.9 percent.
[3] This also excludes 1912 for the Northeast.
[4] For comparability, in calculating House percentages, only percentages for presidential years are included. Results for 1912 are also excluded from these calculations.

percentage of the vote won dropped 8 percentage points in the latter period, from 56.5 to 48.1. The consequence was that the party went from winning an average of 80.3 percent of seats in the Northeast in 1900–28 to 54.3 from 1932–60.

In House elections, the Republican percentages increased in 1952 and 1956, but in 1958, the average percentage dropped to 45.9 and in 1960 to 44.9. The situation did not suggest that the prospects were good for the party in its former stronghold. By 1960 in the Northeast, the party was winning only 30 percent of states in the presidential contest and 52.6 percent of all House seats.

Not only was the overall situation worrisome to Republicans, but it was where the changes were occurring that was troubling to the party. From 1900 to 1928, Republicans had done well in urban areas.[5] Their success in those areas was important because the Northeast was initially much more urban than the rest of the nation, and the presence of urban districts was steadily increasing. In 1900, 39 percent of Northeast districts had high population density (1,000 or more per square mile), while in the rest of the nation, only 9 percent were in that category. By the 1940s, over 60 percent of Northeast House districts were in this category. There was a small decline by 1960, but it was still the case that in the Northeast, 55.3 percent of districts were in the high-density category.

With a majority of northeastern House districts highly urban, the important question was how the party was doing in those districts. Figure 4.1 indicates the percentage of districts won overall and in high-density districts from 1900 to 1960. Prior to 1928, Republicans generally won 60 percent or more of the more urban districts. That success rate was not very different from their overall

5   Samuel J. Eldersveld, "The Influence of Metropolitan Party Pluralities in Presidential Elections since 1920: A Study of Twelve Key Cities," *American Political Science Review* 43 (December, 1949): 1189–1206; Samuel Lubell, *The Future of American Politics*, 2nd ed., Revised (Garden City, NY: Doubleday Anchor Books, 1956); Carl N. Degler, "American Political Parties and the Rise of the City: An Interpretation," *Journal of American History* 51 (June, 1964), 41–59.

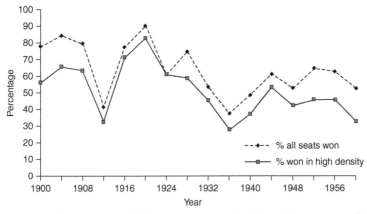

Figure 4.1. Percentage of House seats won by Republicans overall and in high-density districts, Northeast, 1900–60.

success rate. Even in 1928, when Al Smith ran, Republicans still won 60 percent of those districts. Then in 1932, they dropped below 50 percent, winning only 45 percent of high-density districts. The party remained below 50 percent in these districts, except for 1944. With a majority of districts in this category, it brought down the party's overall percentage of districts won and success rate. By 1960, the party was winning only 32.8 percent of seats in the high-density districts, and their overall percentage of seats won was down to 52.6.

The concern for Republicans was whether they could ever win back seats in the highly urban districts. These districts were filled with ethnic immigrants and their offspring and with blacks, many of whom had migrated from the South. Franklin Roosevelt had built a strong connection with urban constituents with various programs to help them during the Great Depression, and that connection appeared to have created a bond that was not likely to erode.[6] Gallup polls in the early 1940s asked about presidential

---

[6] Kristi Andersen, *The Creation of a Democratic Majority 1928–1936* (Chicago: University of Chicago Press, 1979); Lizabeth Cohen, *Making a New Deal: Industrial Workers in Chicago, 1919–1939* (New York: Cambridge University Press, 1990); and David Plotke, *Building a Democratic Political Order: Reshaping American Liberalism in the 1930s and 1940s* (New York: Cambridge University Press, 1996).

preference and classified respondents by socioeconomic status and found that Roosevelt did much better among those with lower incomes.[7] National Election Studies in 1952 and 1956 began the practice of asking with which party the respondents identified. Among those in the Northeast living in central cities, 57 percent identified as Democrat and 36 percent as Republican.[8] In 1958 and 1960, the percentage identifying as Democratic increased to 66. The attachment to the Democratic Party among those in cities seemed strong and unlikely to change. As will be discussed later, there were those within the Northeast who argued that the party could respond to urban needs and do well, but there were reasons for many party members to be skeptical. Attachment to the Democratic Party was strong and growing in northeastern urban areas.

THE ERODING RELEVANCE OF THE NORTHEAST TO REPUBLICAN FORTUNES

Not only had the party lost support in areas where it might be difficult to regain support, but some saw the Northeast as of diminishing importance for the nation and the party. As the rest of the nation grew in population, the Northeast was slowly becoming a smaller percentage of the population. In 1900, 28 percent of the nation lived in the Northeast; by 1960, that percentage was at 25 and declining. The Northeast as a source of votes for Republican presidential candidates was also gradually slipping. As Kevin Phillips pointed out in his analysis of party change, from 1936 to 1960, the percentage of the Republican presidential vote from the Northeast declined from 39.8 to 27.9.[9] The percentage of the total

---

[7] James L. Sundquist, *Dynamics of the Party System*, Revised Ed. (Washington, DC: Brookings Institution Press, 1983), 218.

[8] Source: NES cumulative file. Those who lean to either party are included with those initially identifying with either party.

[9] Kevin P. Phillips, *The Emerging Republican Majority* (New York: Anchor Books, 1970), 184–186. The specific data to support Phillips' analysis were taken from Jerrold G. Rusk, *A Statistical History of the American Electorate* (Washington, DC: CQ Press, 2001), tables 4-4 and 4-5. Though his general point about the decline of the Northeast as a

convention vote for Republican presidential candidates derived from the Northeast was 32.2 in 1940 and 28.4 in 1960.[10] By 1962, the percentage of seats on the Republican National Committee allocated to the Northeast was 20.7.[11] The changes were not great, but they suggested that even if support for Republicans could be recouped in the Northeast, more and more votes for the party were likely to come from elsewhere.

Parties regularly assess their electoral prospects and consider what policy positions might help them. Being in the minority for a lengthy period of time is particularly likely to make a party focus on what it has to do to get out of that situation.[12] The Republican Party was largely in the minority from 1932 through the 1960s. The party was to undergo significant changes in subsequent years. A primary reason the party was willing to at least listen to arguments about why they should change was the evolving situation in the Northeast. The party had lost its solid advantage in the region and its losses were in urban areas dominated by constituencies unlikely to support the party. Moreover, the region was slowly

source of Republican presidential votes and House seats is correct, his specific analysis should be treated with some caution and some interest. In his book he chooses 1936 as the beginning point. That is the year in which Democrats did their best across the nation and left Republicans with largely only their base in the Northeast. That resulted in the Northeast being an abnormally larger percentage of party votes in that year. The same is true for House seats. If the years 1900–60 are examined, 1936 stands out as an abnormal year, so choosing it as a base exaggerates the decline. Phillips also chooses to include only those subsequent years in which a decline occurred and chooses uneven intervals of years for his graph. The result is that his selective use of years and spacing creates an impression of a steady decline after 1936 from a high reliance on the Northeast. The actual decline from 1900 to 1960 is modest, but it is a decline. The interesting matter is that his book is often cited as an important and persuasive argument for why the Republican Party should seek votes elsewhere. His case apparently had an important impact on Richard Nixon, who hired Phillips to work for the administration in 1969 (pp. 22–23). The point is that while his broader argument may have been true, his presentation of evidence about the decline in the Northeast is a distortion of the magnitude and pace of decline.

[10] Rae, *The Decline and Fall of the Liberal Republicans from 1952 to the Present*, 73.
[11] Philip A. Klinkner, *The Losing Parties: Out-Party National Committees, 1956–1993* (New Haven, CT: Yale University Press, 1994), 54.
[12] Marty Cohen, David Karol, Hans Noel, and John Zaller, *The Party Decides: Presidential Nominations Before and After Reform* (Chicago: University of Chicago Press, 2008), 90–92.

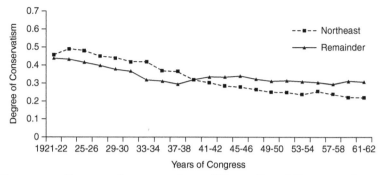

Figure 4.2. Degree of conservatism of House Republican members of Congress, by section, 1921–60.

declining as a relative source of votes within the nation and for the party. There were reasons to consider directing their attention elsewhere. The question was what would be the geographical focus and what would be the message.

THE BATTLE OVER PARTY DIRECTION

Settling on whom to pursue and with what message was not easy. For decades, the base of the party had been the Northeast. The elections of the 1930s resulted in the defeat of many northeastern Republican conservatives in Congress, and their replacement by moderates. The result was that over several decades, the Northeast had switched from being the more conservative wing of the party to the more moderate wing. Indeed, to many conservatives, the delegation of the Northeast was seen as the "liberal" wing of the party. That change was evident in the DW-Nominate scores often used to track the voting positions of members of Congress. Figure 4.2 shows the trend in voting records of Republicans in the Northeast and the rest of the nation.

In the 1920s and 1930s, the northeastern wing of the party was more conservative than the rest of the party. Their party unity scores – the extent to which they voted with the majority of the party – were also higher than those of the rest of the party. Both groups were becoming less conservative, but the Northeast was

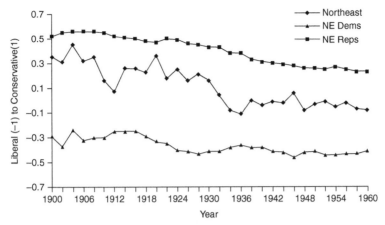

Figure 4.3. Average DW-Nominate scores, House, 1900–60.
Source: Data from Keith Poole, accessed at: http://voteview.com/dwnl.htm

more conservative. Beginning in the 1940s, the relative positions of the two groups reversed, with the northeastern members of the party becoming less conservative than the rest of the party.

This general drift was not well received by conservatives. Their main criticism was that Republicans had largely accepted the expanded role of government adopted by President Roosevelt and the Democrats. In the view of conservatives, with the acquiescence to the New Deal the party had ceased to function as a legitimate conservative alternative to liberal Democrats. To many conservatives, the Northeast wing of the party was the center of this problem.

Conservatives argued that northeastern Republicans were just adapting to Democrats and not presenting an alternative. Figure 4.3 indicates this pattern. From 1900 to 1960, the average Northeast Democratic member of the House was much more liberal (a lower DW-Nominate score) than the average Republican. Democrats as a group had not moved much more liberal over time. The significant change was that the Republicans as a group had moved to become less conservative. To critics, the northeastern wing was largely moving to accommodate Democrats in the region and steadily abandoning the conservative role.

The eastern wing, given the historic concentration of wealth in the Northeast, had been able to dominate fundraising and was seen by many within the party as too dominant in selecting presidential candidates. The conflict between the Northeast and the more conservative wing of the party had manifested itself in the presidential nominating process in the 1940s and the 1950s. In the 1940s, the party chose three nominees from the liberal wing of the party, New Yorkers Wendell Willkie (1940) and Thomas Dewey (1944 and 1948), and repeatedly rejected Robert A. Taft, a conservative Senator from Ohio. When Willkie and Dewey lost the general elections, conservatives were even more frustrated. In 1952, with Dewey not a candidate, conservatives thought they could win the nomination for Taft. The eastern wing, convinced that a conservative could not win, approached Dwight Eisenhower, the general who had presided over the World War II victory, and persuaded him to run. He was seen as a moderate, and his recruitment was seen by conservatives as another case of the liberal eastern wing displacing a conservative who could better represent the party.[13]

Eisenhower's election added to the frustration of conservatives within the party. He was not an opponent of the New Deal, and in the 1952 elections, Eisenhower won 56 percent of the vote outside the South and 48 percent in the South.[14] In 1956, he did even better, winning 59 percent outside the South and 49 percent in the South. Then in the 1958 congressional elections, many Republican conservatives lost and were replaced by liberal Democrats. This further frustrated conservatives and convinced moderates that attracting voters with a conservative message would be very difficult. The northeastern wing was arguing that the party could prosper only by adopting a moderate stance. Eisenhower's victories and the 1958 losses provided support for their arguments.

[13] Rae, *The Decline and Fall of the Liberal Republicans from 1952 to the Present,* 29–35.
[14] Jerrold G. Rusk, *A Statistical History of the American Electorate,* 140.

THE RISE OF THE CONSERVATIVE ARGUMENT

By the end of the 1950s, it appeared to many that the Republican Party had accepted its role as a moderate-to-somewhat-conservative party. Conservatives within the party, however, were not willing to accept that role. There were conservative intellectuals and party activists who wanted the party to challenge the growing role of government in American society.

Conservative activists were inspired by the arguments of such economists as Friedrich Hayek and Milton Friedman, who provided intellectual ballast for the argument that individual freedom and the free market were the basis of a free society, and that liberalism and other forms of statism threatened such liberties.[15] Friedman's argument was that free markets, capitalism, and individualism were essential to freedom and prosperity, and that the growth of government, with its regulations and redistribution, would ultimately squelch these virtues in America. The New Deal growth in government was being too readily accepted. Government was intruding in lives in too many ways and regulating business too much.

Other writers, such as Russell Kirk, were concerned about social order. Kirk railed against the extreme individualism, lack of moral restraints, and lack of social cohesion that they associated with modern liberalism.[16] Conservatives were fundamentally committed to individualism as a virtue. Individuals operating within a competitive capitalistic system should be prodded to do their best, resulting in prosperity for all. Welfare programs of any type undermined individualism. However, individualism did not mean that people could just do as they pleased, which was what liberals were seen as endorsing. The pursuits of individuals had to occur within traditional norms.

---

[15] Friedrich A. Hayek, *The Road to Serfdom* (Chicago: University of Chicago Press, 1944); and Milton Friedman, *Capitalism and Freedom* (Chicago: University of Chicago Press, 1962).
[16] Russell Kirk, *The Conservative Mind from Burke to Santayana* (Chicago: Henry Regnery, 1953).

Tensions between these libertarian and traditionalist strains of modern conservatism were largely resolved by focusing on the common foe, liberalism and other left-of-center ideologies, and on defeating Communism abroad. No one was more central in this endeavor than young William F. Buckley, Jr., who in 1955 founded the weekly *National Review*, which became the sounding board for all strains of modern conservatism. Three years later, the extremely conservative businessman Robert Welch founded the influential John Birch Society, and in 1960, Buckley hosted the founding meeting of Young Americans for Freedom. The conservative movement had taken off.[17] The next step was to give political muscle to the movement by taking over the Republican Party. Anxieties about the direction of America were prompting many conservatives to become activists to counter the troubling liberal trends they saw. They wanted conservatives in power to support conservative values.[18]

CONTENDING VISIONS

It is at junctures such as this that the notion of a "party" response becomes questionable. There is not a party strategy but rather contending forces seeking to shape the future. Differing arguments are put forth by factions, and a struggle ensues for power. Arguments ensue over the viability of different strategies. In this case, there were clear differences of opinion about what to

---

[17] The arguments and efforts of conservatives are detailed in numerous works, such as William A. Rusher, *The Rise of the Right* (New York: Morrow, 1984); Donald Critchlow, *The Conservative Ascendancy* (Cambridge, MA: Harvard University Press, 2007); George H. Nash, *The Conservative Intellectual Movement in America* (New York: Basic Books, 1976); Jerry Z. Muller, Editor, *Conservatism* (Princeton, NJ: Princeton University Press, 1997); Chip Berlet and Matthew S. Lyons, *Right-Wing Populism in America: Too Close for Comfort* (New York: Guilford Press, 2000); John Micklethwait and Adrian Wooldridge, *The Right Nation: Conservative Power in America* (New York: Penguin Press, 2004); and Jerome Himmelstein, *To the Right: The Transformation of American Conservatism* (Berkeley, CA: University of California Press, 1990).

[18] Lisa McGirr, *Suburban Warriors* (Princeton, NJ: Princeton University Press, 2002), 54–110. For a recent analysis of the rise of concern about traditional values, see Marc J. Hetherington and Jonathan Weiler, *Authoritarianism and Polarization in American Politics* (New York: Cambridge University Press, 2009).

do. The more moderate northeastern wing of the party hoped to improve their fortunes in urban areas in their region. Some thought that the result of President Eisenhower sending troops to Little Rock, Arkansas in 1957 to enforce integration rulings would be greater support from blacks in northern urban areas and continuing conflict over race within the Democratic Party.[19] Some within the Republican National Committee were convinced that the problem was reestablishing Republican organizations in northern cities. In the battle for the 1960 nomination for president, Richard Nixon was so convinced of the need to accommodate the liberal wing of the party that he left the convention in Chicago and flew to New York City to negotiate an agreement on issues with New York Governor Nelson Rockefeller, a move that angered conservatives.[20] After Nixon lost the 1960 election, analyses indicated that he lost several northern states (Delaware, New Jersey, and Pennsylvania) by small margins and New York by only five percentage points. Since the 1960 election had been so close, it would take only modest gains in northern cities to swing the next presidential election to Republicans. A study done in 1961 found that many cities had no party organization. Republicans were losing large cities and winning the rest of large swing states, and the argument was that greater efforts in cities might help them overcome weaknesses there. If local organizations were revived they could mount get-out-the-vote efforts and monitor problems of ballot fraud that might be helping Democrats.[21] In short, there were those who thought the party could win subsequent elections by focusing on northern states.

There were also efforts to create a vehicle to articulate moderate party positions. Senators from the Northeast sought to form a party policy council to formulate party positions.[22] In May 1961,

[19] W. H. Lawrence, "G.O.P. Hopes for a Big Negro Vote," *New York Times* (October 6, 1957), 199; W. H. Lawrence, "G.O.P. to Cite Little Rock, Minimize 'Moon' in '58 Bid," *New York Times* (October 16, 1957), 1.
[20] Rae, *The Decline and Fall of Liberal Republicans*, 42.
[21] Klinkner, *The Losing Parties*, 41–47.
[22] Ibid., 65.

former president Dwight Eisenhower convened a Republican Citizens' Committee at his Gettysburg home. This collection of prominent moderates sought to establish a moderate image for the party.[23] However, none of these efforts had much impact within the party.

Conservative Republicans saw a different future for the party. They wanted to pursue other voters. To them, the evidence suggested that the losses in the Northeast were sustained and primarily among urban voters who were unlikely to return to the party. Conservatives also disliked the ideological dominance of northeastern moderates within the party and were not inclined to take actions bolstering that wing of the party. Instead, they saw the future of the party in the South. They saw evidence that the party could succeed in the South, whose voters would be more receptive to their appeals than the Northeast. Strom Thurmond's third-party candidacy in 1948, in reaction against the sympathy for civil rights emerging from President Truman and the northern wing of the Democratic Party, had prompted many southerners to defect from the Democratic Party in the presidential race.[24] In 1952, the Republican national chairman visited the South and, in a speech in Atlanta, expressed the party's support for states' rights.[25] In the 1952 and 1956 elections, Eisenhower almost got 50 percent of the southern vote. There were indications that the South would respond positively to a Republican message of restraining the national government.

The challenge was to capitalize on this possibility. The Republican National Committee (RNC) made its first organized efforts to act on this in 1957 when it established Operation Dixie. Southern state party organizations had always existed and had a formal organizational role within the party, but their ideological impact within the party was limited. For decades, the party had been allocating seats

[23] Ibid., 64–68.
[24] Harvard Sitkoff, "Harry Truman and the Election of 1948: The Coming of Age of Civil Rights in American Politics," *Journal of Southern History*, 37 (1971), 597–616.
[25] Joseph Lowndes, *From the New Deal to the New Right: Race and the Southern Origins of Modern Conservatism* (New Haven, CT: Yale University Press, 2008), 36.

on the RNC according to a formula of two members per state plus a bonus one if the state had voted Republican in the last presidential race.[26] This gave the South roughly 25 percent of the seats on the RNC. The South was also allocated about the same percentage of votes at the national conventions to nominate presidential candidates.[27] This allocation of voting rights, however, had done little to generate votes or to sway the direction of the party. The South regularly provided a smaller percentage of national Republican votes than its allocation of convention votes.[28] Perhaps more importantly, southern delegates tended to split their vote much like the rest of the nation, resulting in the region having no influence on the candidates chosen by the party.[29]

The role of the South within the party was soon to change, however. In the 1950s, most state organizations in the South were barely active. As a result of Operation Dixie, the party was able to build up county organizations in the South and recruit more middle-class, conservative activists.[30] By 1961, the RNC was allocating more money to efforts in the South and in 1962 the party began distributing a regular newsletter in the region.

Despite these efforts, the relevance of the South within the party was slow in coming. In the 1960 election, the battle for the Republican presidential nomination was between Vice-President Richard Nixon and New York Governor Nelson Rockefeller. Rockefeller, coming from a relatively liberal northeastern state, had become governor by advocating an activist government. In an effort to accommodate Rockefeller, whom Nixon saw as his main challenger, the Vice-President traveled to New York City during the convention and agreed to what became known as the Fifth Avenue Compact, accepting many of Rockefeller's positions, including a more liberal civil rights platform.[31] Conservatives did

[26] Rae, *The Decline and Fall of Liberal Republicans*, 68.
[27] Ibid., 73.
[28] Klinkner, *The Losing Parties,* 50.
[29] Ibid., 69.
[30] Ibid., 51–52.
[31] Rick Perlstein, *Nixonland*, 50; and Klinkner, *The Losing Parties*, 52.

not like either Nixon or Rockefeller, and Nixon's capitulation to Rockefeller severely disappointed them. Arizona Senator Barry Goldwater compared the Fifth Avenue Compact to the appeasement of Adolf Hitler at Munich. Afterward Nixon lost the 1960 election by the narrowest of margins, carrying only four Southern states (Florida, Kentucky, Tennessee, and Virginia). To conservatives, the party was in the worst possible situation, in the minority and without a clear identity. It needed another strategy and it had to decide where to pursue voters.

As argued earlier, the conservative wing believed that the future of the party was in the South. As Barry Goldwater, Senator from Arizona, put it in a 1961 statement to southern Republican state party chairmen: "We're not going to get the Negro vote as a bloc in 1964 and 1968, so we ought to go hunting where the ducks are."[32] Goldwater was not alone in believing that the future of the party depended on success in the South. Brent Bozell, a conservative commentator, argued that:

> ... a successful appeal to the South is the *sine qua non* for beating John F. Kennedy in 1964 – indeed, that pursuit of such a strategy over the long term is the party's only realistic hope of escaping from the Hobson's choice of throwing itself on the mercy of an Eisenhower-type personality cult, or accepting national minority status.[33]

Conservatives' presumption was that the best vehicle for pursuing the South was a presidential candidacy. Such a figure could redefine the party. The issue was whether such a strategy was feasible. Did it make sense to focus on that region and was it really feasible to make gains in the South? Would such an emphasis cost them votes in the Northeast? The challenge for conservatives was to convince others that another strategy would work for the party.

The conservatives within the party were not just engaging in wishful thinking. They had analyzed election results and had a

---

[32] Klinkner, *The Losing Parties*, 58.
[33] L. Brent Bozell, "Goldwater for President: Is it Feasible?" *National Review* (April 23, 1963), 313.

plan about how to create a majority. William Rusher, publisher of *National Review*, made a detailed case for pursuing the South. He had three main points.[34] The first was that while moderates and "practiced pragmatists" thought it was necessary to win the large industrial states, his view was that the party's prospects were not good there. Moderate governors were not winning in those states, there was little evidence of support for Republicans, and staking the future of the party on these states was not a good bet. Second, winning the South was feasible. The South had been a lock for Democrats, but the region was changing, becoming more of a "modern mixed economy," and the emergence of national magazines and television were breaking down its isolation. It was also voting more Republican. Eisenhower had done well in the South in 1952 and 1956, winning almost 50 percent of the vote and several states. There was evidence to support Rusher's interpretation. Southern Republicans recruited more candidates to run in the South in 1962. These candidates were stressing states' rights and expressing empathy for southerners opposed to federal desegregation initiatives. In the 1962 House elections, Republicans won 31 percent of all votes cast in the South, an increase from the 16.3 percent won in 1958. The number of House seats being contested by Republicans was steadily increasing, rising from 35 percent of all seats in 1958 to 67 percent in 1962.[35] The RNC found hope in the results and allocated more money to efforts within the region.[36]

Third, tensions within the Democratic Party provided an opportunity for Republicans to exploit. The party was trying to please northern liberals and southern segregationists, an impossible task.[37] As Frank Meyer, another prominent conservative, put it: "Johnson faces an insoluble dilemma. He cannot at one and the

[34] William A. Rusher, "Crossroads for the G.O.P.," *National Review* (February 12, 1963), 109–112.
[35] Mark D. Brewer and Jeffrey M. Stonecash, *Dynamics of American Political Parties*, 110–113.
[36] Klinkner, *The Losing Parties*, 56–57.
[37] Rusher, "Crossroads for the G.O.P.," 111.

same time satisfy both the South and the Northern Liberal and Negro leaders."[38]

The issue was how could Republicans capitalize on Democratic tensions? The Democratic coalition "can be brought crashing to the ground, but not by another 'me-too' Republican campaign."[39] "...[T]hey [the South] are calling for a conservative GOP and a conservative presidential candidate." The prime candidate was Barry Goldwater:[40] ".... Goldwater is the only Republican candidate who can exploit those [the Democratic Party's North-South conflict] and bring victory to the Republican Party in November."[41]

Conservatives were not unaware of the risks of this strategy, but for various reasons they were untroubled by it. Rusher anticipated that pursuit of the South would lead to the charge that "any Republican concession to Southern sentiment is a venture in sheer racism, and will lose the GOP crucial votes in the North and West."[42] He did not think this was a risk because the Democratic Party was too entangled in its own divisions about race to credibly make that charge against a Republican Party that had fewer segregationists in it. He also doubted that the North would be willing to embrace the Democratic Party:

> Certainly there is not a shred of evidence that any large bloc of votes now sustaining Republican dominance in any northern or western state will bolt to the party of Kennedy (and Eastland and Ellender [segregationist Southern Senators]) because the GOP chooses to bid vigorously for the support of the new middle class of a changing south.[43]

Some thought that while a conservative like Goldwater might win the Northeast, those votes were unnecessary for a victory. If a

---

[38] Frank S. Meyer, "Principles and Heresies: And Still ... Goldwater Can Win," *National Review* (December 17, 1963), 528.

[39] Frank S. Meyer, "Principles and Heresies: Why Goldwater Can Defeat Johnson," *National Review* (July 14, 1964), 581.

[40] James J. Kilpatrick, "Goldwater Country," *National Review* (April 9, 1963), 281–282.

[41] Meyer, "Why Goldwater Can Defeat Johnson," 581.

[42] Rusher, "Crossroads for the G.O.P.," 111.

[43] Ibid., 112.

conservative could win most of the Midwest, the Mountain states, some Southern Border states, and California or Texas, victory could be secured.[44] Others were clearly eager to pursue a conservative direction, were frustrated by the continuing dominance of the eastern liberal wing, and were ready to displace the influence of the Northeast within the party.[45] For various reasons, there was a base within the party willing to pursue voters outside the Northeast.

While various factions were arguing about what direction the party should take, conservatives were organizing to secure the nomination for their candidate in the 1964 presidential race. The party was once again going to face the issue of whether to nominate a moderate or conservative in 1964. Conservatives set out to secure the nomination for Barry Goldwater.[46] Their efforts were focused and systematic. They developed lists of conservatives across the nation and sought to recruit them to positions in state party organizations and make them influential at a time when a majority of national convention votes came from state delegations chosen by state party organizations and not from state primaries.[47] After a long and bruising preconvention campaign, in which they had to fend off the candidacy of relatively liberal New York Governor Nelson Rockefeller, their efforts paid off.[48] Perhaps most important, the efforts to mobilize conservative support within the South paid off, with Goldwater winning 97.1 percent of all delegates from that region.[49]

[44] Frank S. Meyer, "Principles and Heresies: A New Political Map," *National Review* (August 11, 1964), 687.
[45] Rae, *The Decline and Fall of Liberal Republicans,* 25–53; and McGirr, *Suburban Warriors,* 91–98.
[46] Rick Perlstein, *Before the Storm* (New York: Hill and Wang, 2001).
[47] Rae, *The Decline of Liberal Republicans,* 54–59. Over time the party changed its delegate selection process from state conventions to party primary votes (124), but in 1964 it was possible to focus on securing support within state party processes and secure a large number of convention delegates.
[48] Richard Perlstein, *Before the Storm,* 158–180.
[49] Klinkner, *The Losing Parties,* 69.

GOLDWATER AS THE REPRESENTATIVE
OF THE REPUBLICAN PARTY

Conservatives had sought for years to have a spokesman for their cause and they finally had one in Goldwater. The important matter was what he stood for and how he would be received in the Northeast. In *The Conscience of a Conservative*,[50] Goldwater articulated his commitment to conservatism, the propriety of free markets, and the fundamental importance of individual and states' rights to the preservation of freedom. He criticized high levels of federal taxing and spending, the New Deal welfare state, and federal involvement in education. He challenged the validity of continuing Social Security. Perhaps most forcefully, Goldwater argued vehemently that the Soviet Union was the ultimate threat to the United States and that the nation must defeat the Soviets by any means necessary, including the use of nuclear weapons. In his acceptance speech at the Republican national convention he also issued his famous statement that "extremism in the defense of liberty is no vice, and moderation in the pursuit of justice is no virtue." The campaign of Barry Goldwater presented Americans with a clear statement of conservative principles. To his followers he was a crucial figure.[51]

To many others, however, the move to a conservative message and the nomination of Goldwater was dangerous. To moderates within the party, at a time in which there appeared to be a consensus that government could address many major social problems, Goldwater was bucking that trend, arguing that government did too much, should not address social problems, and that there would be negative effects from these efforts. At a time when there were fears of nuclear weapons, he suggested that we should not be afraid to engage in their limited use.

Among politicians in the Northeast, his positions were seen as detrimental to the future of the party. Jacob Javits, the moderate

---

[50] Shepherdsville, KY: Victor Pub. Co., 1960.
[51] McGirr, *Suburban Warriors*, 111–146.

Senator from New York, argued that moving in the direction of Goldwater would polarize the parties along ideological lines and make the party less of a national party. His fear was that the Southern Strategy of states' rights "could result most likely in the election-day loss of many of the great industrial and urban states of the North ..." "A candidacy based upon the 'Southern Strategy' ... would do more than hazard the party's defeat in the 1964 contest; it could alienate millions of Americans – who could stay alienated for years ..."[52] The northeastern wing was strongly opposed to his candidacy,[53] and many politicians within the region sought to separate themselves from Goldwater during their campaigns.[54] The concern was that the positions of Barry Goldwater would define the image of the Republican Party within the Northeast, to the party's detriment.

THE DEMOCRATIC ALTERNATIVE

The question for voters was what Democrats represented as an alternative. The emergence of a truly conservative Republican candidate occurred at a time of considerable change and uncertainty for Democrats, who were facing their own difficulties in trying to construct a coalition to win the presidency. The very trends in the South that so encouraged conservative Republicans were worrisome to Democratic strategists. The addition of northern urban areas to the party coalition had created a less cohesive party.

Tensions within the party that Republicans sought to exploit were real. The non-southern wing of the Democratic Party had won more seats following the 1932 and 1936 elections and constituted a greater proportion of the party. Pressures were emerging from these states for action on civil rights issues. Democratic state

---

[52] Jacob K. Javits, "'To Preserve the Two-Party System'," *New York Times Magazine* (October 27, 1963), 15+.

[53] Rae, *The Decline and Fall of Liberal Republicans*, 61–64.

[54] Warren Weaver, "Goldwater's Candidacy Stirs Fears of Republicans in Northeast; Wary of Joint Campaign; Guarantee Is Sought; Difficulties in Connecticut," *New York Times* (June 30, 1963), 28; John H. Fenton, "Massachusetts Republicans, Cool to Goldwater, Will Stress State Issues in Campaign," *New York Times* (July 22, 1964), 15.

party platforms outside the South were becoming much more
supportive of civil rights policies than Republicans.[55] By the mid-
1940s, non-southern Democrats in the House of Representatives
were making efforts to get civil rights legislation considered by
signing discharge petitions and making speeches on the floor.[56] In
1948, President Harry Truman had announced several executive
orders to eliminate racial segregation in the federal agencies.[57]
The 1948 national convention adopted a plank on this issue more
liberal than ever before.

This willingness of the Democratic Party to openly support civil
rights prompted Democratic Senator Strom Thurmond of South
Carolina to run for the presidency in 1948 on a third-party line,
taking large chunks of votes away from Truman in the South.
Support for Democratic candidates never returned to pre-1948
levels, and by the early 1960s, it was clear that the party could no
longer count on that region. In 1948, Truman lost four states to
Thurmond. The Democratic presidential candidate in 1952 and
1956 was Adlai Stevenson, and he lost four (and another four were
close) and six (and another one was close), respectively, of the
southern states. Democratic presidential candidates realized they
had to increase their vote outside the South.[58]

At the same time, the prospects for gains in northern urban
areas seemed to be improving. Further gains in those areas
could provide enough of a margin in some states to secure the
Electoral College votes in those states and offset possible losses in
the South. The party had done better in northern cities for some
time with its message of limiting government imposition of moral

[55] Brian D. Feinstein and Eric Schickler, "Platforms and Partners: The Civil Rights
Realignment Reconsidered," *Studies in American Political Development*, 22 (Spring
2008), 115–116.
[56] Eric Schickler, Kathryn Pearson, and Brian D. Feinstein, "Shifting Partisan
Coalitions: Support for Civil Rights in Congress from 1933–1972," *Journal of Politics*,
forthcoming.
[57] Michael Gardner, *Harry Truman and Civil Rights: Moral Courage and Political Risks*
(Carbondale, IL: Southern Illinois University Press, 2003).
[58] Alan Ware, *The Democratic Party Heads North, 1877–1962* (New York: Cambridge
University Press, 2006), 1–15 and 274.

codes and sympathy to urban immigrants. This appealed because immigrants disliked political efforts to limit immigration, restrict Catholic schools, and impose prohibition.[59] The party made further and sustained gains in the 1930s in northern cities. In the 1960 presidential race, Kennedy was able to win twenty-seven of the thirty-nine largest cities.[60] The party's success in the north was fragile, however, and created uncertainty about the prospects for winning these states.[61]

The prospects and dangers of appealing to urban areas had increased in recent decades because of a steady stream of blacks migrating from the South in search of northern urban jobs.[62] Blacks were now a greater presence in these areas and could provide the margin to secure a majority in many states. Democrats increased their number of congressional seats in the 1958 elections, and most of those winning were liberals. John F. Kennedy won in 1960 and spoke of a New Frontier, involving many liberal policies. He was concerned with poverty and with increasing programs to promote equality of opportunity.[63] It appeared that support for liberal policies was on the rise.[64]

The most contentious issue that the Democratic president and his party faced was civil rights. Activists from non-southern states were continuing to push for more civil rights policies,[65] and their representatives in Congress were becoming more vocal in support.[66] The difficulty was that strong stands on civil rights would likely cost any Democratic candidate all southern states. However, since the South was sliding away from the party, it might

---

[59] John K. White, *The Fractured Electorate* (Hanover, NH: University Press of New England, 1983), 9; and Ware, *The Democratic Party Heads North*, 26.

[60] Carl N. Degler, "American Political Parties and the Rise of the City: An Interpretation," *Journal of American History* 51 (June 1964), 58.

[61] Ware, *The Democratic Party Heads North*, 43.

[62] Nicholas Lemann, *The Promised Land* (New York: Alfred A. Knopf, 1991).

[63] Daniel Knapp and Kenneth Polk, *Scouting the War on Poverty: Social Reform Politics in the Kennedy Administration* (Lexington, MA: Heath Lexington Books, 1971).

[64] G. Calvin Mackenzie and Robert Weisbrot, *The Liberal Hour: Washington and the Politics of Change in the 1960s* (New York: Penguin Press, 2008).

[65] Feinstein and Schickler, "Platforms and Partners," 11–12 and 15–18.

[66] Schickler, Pearson, and Feinstein, "Shifting Partisan Coalitions."

be that a presidential candidate had to make an appeal involving civil rights. The national party was trying to cope with dis-
agreement by negotiating compromises between the southern and
non-southern wings on this issue.

At the same time, the pressures for action were increasing as
the civil rights movement grew.[67] The number of marches pro-
testing the treatment of blacks in the South was increasing and
were being met with violent resistance, which was broadcast on the
nightly news. In August 1963, Martin Luther King gave his "I Have
a Dream" speech in Washington. Following the assassination of
Kennedy in November 1963, Lyndon Johnson became president
and quickly moved to support a strong civil rights bill and numerous other liberal programs.[68] The issue presented one of the great
moral dilemmas and dramas of American politics. Blacks had been
denied multiple rights for decades and were peacefully petition-
ing for those rights. Northern liberals were adamantly pushing
for legislation to establish those rights, and Southern Democrats
in the Senate were reading telephone books aloud as they filibus-
tered the legislation in an effort to preserve segregation in the
South and fend off federal action. Lyndon Johnson was pushing
the legislation for moral and practical reasons. He apparently was
not only convinced that the time had come for change, but that
that the future of the Democratic Party was with liberals outside
of the South, including blacks.[69] In a May 1964 speech, Johnson
announced his Great Society program. The Democratic president
was clearly staking out a position of sympathy to black interests.

At the same time, Republicans had come to their own crossroads on civil rights. The national Republican Party had an image
of being more supportive of civil rights than Democrats, but this

[67] Taylor Branch, *Parting the Waters: America in the King Years* (New York: Simon and
   Schuster, 1989).
[68] Sidney M. Milkis, "Lyndon Johnson, the Great Society, and the Modern Presidency,"
   in Sidney M. Milkis and Jerome M. Mileur, eds., *The Great Society and the High Tide of
   Liberalism* (Amherst, MA: University of Massachusetts Press, 2006), 1–49.
[69] William E. Leuchtenburg, *The White House Looks South* (Baton Rouge, LA: Louisiana
   State University Press, 2005).

relative image was largely because the Democratic Party contained so many southerners opposed to change.[70] Northern Democrats were very supportive. Within the Republican Party there were many, as noted before, who thought that a stance in favor of states' rights and opposition to federal desegregation efforts made ideological and political sense as a way to make inroads in the South. It was also the case that within most non-southern states, Republicans had been expressing in state platforms considerably less support for civil rights legislation than Democrats.[71] Both parties were experiencing change.

While the national battle over civil rights legislation was playing out, Barry Goldwater announced that he was voting against the 1964 Civil Rights bill. He made an effort to indicate that he was not in favor of segregation and the denial of rights, arguing that his stance was based on general opposition to federal intrusion into state and local matters.[72] He was, however, plagued by past statements such as those indicating that he thought the 1954 Supreme Court decision requiring desegregation "… was right. But I don't think it is necessarily the supreme law of the land." He supported states' rights and said in 1961 that "I would bend every muscle to see that the South has a voice on everything that affects the life of the South."[73] Despite his efforts to establish a principled basis for opposition, his stance was widely simplified into opposition to civil

[70] Edward G. Carmines and James A. Stimson, *Issue Evolution* (Princeton, NJ: Princeton University Press, 1989), 64–78, though Feinstein and Schickler document that in non-southern state party platforms, Democrats were much more supportive than Republicans. Republican members of Congress were also less willing to advocate for civil rights. See Schickler, Pearson, and Feinstein, "Shifting Partisan Coalitions." The significance is that while the Republican Party had an official voting record in Congress of being more supportive of civil rights than Democrats, the party was experiencing far less pressure than Democrats to support civil rights.

[71] Feinstein and Schickler, "Platforms and Partners." For a discussion of the transition of views within the Republican Party, see Shamira M. Gelbman and Jesse H. Rhodes, "Why Didn't Republicans Adopt Racial Conservativism Earlier?" presented at the 2010 Southern Political Science Association Meetings, Atlanta, Georgia, January.

[72] Perlstein, *Before the Storm*, 363–364.

[73] "Goldwater Solicits G.O.P. Votes from Southern Segregationists," *New York Times* (November 19, 1961), 70.

rights and part of an effort to appeal to the South.[74] By the end of
the campaign, Goldwater was commonly labeled as very conservative, opposed to social welfare legislation, civil rights, and an
activist federal government, skeptical about Social Security, and
willing to be much more aggressive in foreign affairs.

[74] Perlstein, *Before the Storm*, 266–267, 426–428, 507–510.

CHAPTER 5

Interpreting the Goldwater Election and Pursuing the South

The results of the 1964 election were clear, but their interpretation was not, and the differing views reflected the growing split within the Republican Party. Lyndon Johnson received 61.1 percent of the national popular vote and House Democratic candidates received 57.4 percent of the national vote. Democrats won 26 of 33 Senate contests. The loss was seen by many as a disaster for Republicans. Goldwater's position had apparently defined the party to many voters and they did not like what they heard. As James Reston of *The New York Times* put it, "He has wrecked his party for a long time to come." Another columnist wrote, "The election has finished the Goldwater school of political reaction."[1] There were immediate efforts to replace the conservative party leadership that Goldwater had brought in.[2]

The election had a devastating effect within the Northeast. In the elections from 1954 through 1962, Republicans had won an average of 54.7 percent of House seats within the region, ranging from 49.1 percent to 62.9 percent. Following the 1964 election, the party held 36.7 percent of House seats, lower than their prior low of 37.4 percent in 1936. Goldwater averaged 31.2 percent of the vote in northeastern House districts and lost all ten states by wide margins. There were nine Senate seats up for election in the region, and Republicans won only two of them, both by small

[1] Rick Perlstein, *Before the Storm* (New York: Hill and Wang, 2001), ix.
[2] Ibid., 512–516.

margins. There was little positive news in the results for northeastern Republicans.

Moderates within the party argued that a continued focus on the
Southern Strategy was of questionable morality and just would not
work. The Ripon Society, founded in 1962[3] to advocate moderate
positions, exemplified these views. Their editors found attempts to
appeal to southern opposition to the civil rights movement "sad,
shameful, and a collapse of courage."[4] They also argued that the
numbers were against the strategy, citing the "decisive Negro vote
of 1964," the growing black vote both North and South, the lack
of party strength where the black population was high, and the
party's failure to appeal to urban voters.[5] The editors of the Ripon
Society went further, arguing that the party had to recognize the
growing urban nature of America and appeal to voters in those
areas.[6]

There was evidence to support their analysis, at least in the
Northeast. By 1964, 28.3 percent of the nation's House districts
had a density of 1,000 people per square mile or greater. In
the Northeast, 46.8 percent of House districts were in this category. Within those high-density districts, as Figure 5.1 indicates,
Democrats were doing very well. In those districts, Democrats won
78.4 percent of seats in 1964 and in the moderate density districts
they also won a majority of seats, 57.4 percent, the first time the
party had won a majority in that category. Further the initial evidence from voting analyses did not indicate that the party had

[3]   As expressed on their web page, the Ripon Society was founded "in 1962 to revive
      the Grand Old Party's commitment to inclusion and reform. Founded on the values
      of Abraham Lincoln and Teddy Roosevelt, Ripon believes in their legacy of innova-
      tion, equality of opportunity for all people, mutual responsibility, and self-govern-
      ment. The Ripon Society was the first major Republican Party [sic] to support the
      passage of the Civil Rights Bill in the 1960s." http://www.riponsociety.org/history.
      htm. See also Howard L. Reiter, "Ripon: Left Spur to the GOP," *The Nation* (February
      17, 1969), 202–205.
[4]   [Editors] "The View from Here," *The Ripon Forum,* 1, no. 4 (June 1965), 1.
[5]   [Editors] "Republicans and the Negro Revolution – 1965," *The Ripon Forum,* 1, no. 8
      (December 1965), 1; [Editors] "Republicans and the South," *The Ripon Forum* 1, no.
      3 (May 1965), 2; and [Editors] "The State of the Democratic Coalition: The Maginot
      Line," *The Ripon Forum* 11, no. 4 (June 1966), 5.
[6]   [Editors] "The State of the Democratic Coalition: The Maginot Line," 5.

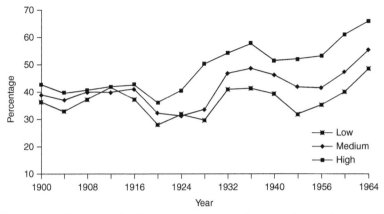

Figure 5.1. Democratic House percentages by population density of districts, Northeast, 1900–64.

benefited from any white urban backlash in northern cities.[7] The moderates were arguing that blacks were going to become more important, and that the party was losing them. Opposition to civil rights was not creating greater support among whites, prompting the chairman of the Republican National Committee (RNC) to argue that the party had to be careful about appearing to be racist.[8]

Despite the array of analysts who saw a serious setback for the conservative cause, conservatives saw the results as a reason for optimism. William Rusher of *National Review* had argued that the party could succeed in the South, and Goldwater did win five Southern states – Alabama, Georgia, Louisiana, Mississippi, and South Carolina.[9] In 1961, Goldwater famously stated that if Republicans wanted to gain votes, they needed "to go hunting where the ducks

[7] Anthony Lewis, "White Backlash Doesn't Develop," *New York Times* (November 4, 1964), 1.
[8] John D. Morris, "Burch Asks G.O.P. to Reject Racism," *New York Times* (February 18, 1965), 18.
[9] For a discussion on the importance of this, see Bernard Cosman, *Five States for Goldwater: Continuity and Change in Southern Presidential Voting Patterns* (University, AL: University of Alabama Press, 1966); David Lublin, *The Republican South: Democratization and Partisan Change* (Princeton, NJ: Princeton University Press, 2004).

are," and Goldwater and many of his conservative supporters saw plenty of ducks in the South. While some saw the assessment as grasping, it was the first time the party received more electoral votes in the South (37) than outside the South (15). The party increased its number of House seats in the South from 11 to 16. In 1950, the party had 35 candidates for the 114 seats in that region. Those 35 averaged 27.3 percent of the vote. In 1964, they had 81 candidates who averaged 38.6 percent. The party was making inroads, and many conservatives wanted to continue to pursue the South.

While the battle over the direction of the party continued, events and the imperatives of the presidential election came to play a major role. The 1964 election took place amid great concern for civil rights. As 1964, 1965, and 1966 unfolded, urban riots became more commonplace. Liberals such as Lyndon Johnson were dismayed that the many programs he was enacting were not solving the problem but were accompanied by anger and riots.[10] Crime was increasing and protests about Vietnam were becoming larger and getting more attention. To many, events seemed out of control and social order seemed to be crumbling.[11] The elections of 1966 were dominated by discussions of "backlash," or negative reactions to all of these events.[12] The election produced significant gains for Republicans, who gained forty-four House seats. Ronald Reagan, who had established himself during the Goldwater campaign as an eloquent advocate of conservative principles, was elected governor of California. The 1966 election fundamentally altered the situation of Republican House incumbents. Ever since the 1932 landslide for Democrats, Republican incumbents had been struggling to achieve the same level of electoral success that Democrats enjoyed. From 1946 through 1964, 70.9 percent, on average, of Democrats had safe seats, defined as seats won with 60 percent or more of the vote. During

[10] Perlstein provides a valuable summary of the chronology of events in *Nixonland: The Rise of a President and the Fracturing of America* (New York: Scribner, 2007), 96–127.
[11] Perlstein, *Nixonland*, 274–278.
[12] Thomas B. Edsall and Mary D. Edsall, *Chain Reaction: The Impact of Race, Rights, and Taxes on American Politics* (New York: W.W. Norton, 1991).

that time, only 43.6 percent of Republicans achieved vote percentages of that level or more. In the 1966 elections, 89.2 percent of Republican incumbents in the House were safe, while the success of Democratic incumbents declined.[13] For the first time in decades, Republican incumbents were achieving the electoral success of Democrats.

Their success in the South was particularly important. The party ran 66 candidates in the South in 1966 and they averaged 47.3 percent of the vote. If the number of seats is compared to 1962, the party had gone from 55 to 46 seats in the Northeast and from 13 to 26 seats in the South. In the remainder of the nation, the number increased from 113 to 119. These southern gains and northeastern losses further convinced many that the party's future was not in the Northeast.[14]

Perhaps most important was the imperative of the pending presidential election. Candidates needed to figure out where they could win enough states to win a plurality or majority in the Electoral College. Richard Nixon, following the losses of the presidential race in 1960 and the California governorship in 1962, was seeking to make a comeback. He was faced with the ongoing efforts of Nelson Rockefeller, governor of New York, to secure the nomination. Nixon had also come to realize how important the South was in trying to secure the presidential nomination. The South had 279 of the necessary 655 votes at the 1964 convention and would have more in 1968 because convention votes were weighted according to recent success. Since Goldwater had done so well in 1964 in the South, that region would have more votes in 1968.[15] But Nixon also knew that northeastern states had a long history of voting Republican, as long as he did not alienate voters there.[16]

[13] Jeffrey M. Stonecash, *Reassessing the Incumbency Effect* (New York: Cambridge University Press, 2009).
[14] M. Stanton Evans, "Conservatives, Si," *The National Review* (November 1, 1966), 1091–1093.
[15] Perlstein, *Nixonland*, 88.
[16] [Editors] "Republican Arithmetic," *The National Review* 4, no. 8 (August, 1968), 9–12.

During the next two years, Nixon sought to position himself as sympathetic to southern concerns but not so sympathetic that he would not enforce desegregation laws. He voiced his opposition to legal segregation but indicated that he did not think it wise for the federal government to dictate solutions.[17] He wanted to appeal to the South but had to be careful about not alienating northern states where support for desegregation was greater. He watched the success Ronald Reagan had in California by denouncing urban riots, campus protests, and crime in general, and argued that the "silent majority" wanted social order and that he would enforce the laws.[18] He claimed to have a secret plan to end the Vietnam War, which he could not reveal. The presidential election campaign was a difficult one because of the presence of George Wallace, the segregationist former governor of Alabama, who threatened to win many southern states and negate the logic of Nixon focusing on the South. Ultimately Nixon won a very close race, with 43.4 percent of the popular vote. He won Florida, Kentucky, North Carolina, South Carolina, Tennessee, and Virginia, giving him forty-five Electoral College votes in the South, more than Goldwater received, despite the presence of Wallace.

Equally important, Nixon was able to win the presidency with only four states within the Northeast – Delaware, New Hampshire, New Jersey, and Vermont. In House elections, the party recovered somewhat from the low of 1964 but was still only able to win 44 percent of the seats within the region. Democrats won three of the five northeastern Senate elections that year.

The crucial issue for Republicans was the shifting importance of the regions of the nation for the future of the party. Again there are always contending views within a party,[19] with some arguing

---

[17] David S. Broder, "Nixon, in the South, Bids G.O.P. Drop Race Issue," *New York Times* (May 7, 1966), 14.
[18] Matthew D. Lassiter, *The Silent Majority: Suburban Politics in the Sunbelt South* (Princeton, NJ: Princeton University Press, 2007).
[19] Phillips's analysis was met with a strong dissent by the editors of the Ripon Society. See their critique of the book: "It's Not that Simple," *Ripon Forum*, 5, no. 10 (October 1969), 9–20.

that a moderate could win.[20] Perhaps the most interesting argument was that made by a budding young analyst, Kevin Phillips, who provided a conservative roadmap for where Nixon might want to take the party. He had worked for the Nixon campaign and published his analysis after Nixon's election. While Phillips asserted that the book "does *not* purport to set forth the past strategies or future intentions of Richard M. Nixon, his campaign organization or administration," it was difficult not to see it in that light. His argument proved to be prescient about what would happen in subsequent years.[21]

Phillips argued that "the Northeast ... is the final bastion of *status quo* liberalism" "with the Eastern Establishment Republicans in the vanguard" and that the "... emerging Republican majority of the Nineteen-Seventies is centered in the South, the West, and in the 'Middle-American' urban-suburban districts." He saw the Republican Party as steadily increasing its "... reliance [on the] South and West since the beginning of the New Deal cycle in 1932."[22] Perhaps most important, he felt that "... the 1964 election constituted a Rubicon for the Republican Party; and its crossing marked off an era."[23] "The Republican Party shed the dominion of its Yankee and Northeast Establishment creators, while the Democrats, having linked themselves to the Negro socioeconomic revolution and to an increasingly liberal Northeastern Establishment shaped by the success of the New Deal, sank the foundations of their future into the Northeast."[24]

[20] Howard Reiter, "The Collapsing Coalitions," *Ripon Forum* (November 1968), 7–15.
[21] Kevin Phillips, *The Emerging Republican Majority* (New York: Anchor Books, 1970), 21; emphasis in the original.
[22] Ibid., 23 and 26. While Phillips denied wanting to write off the Northeast, one reviewer summarized his argument as follows: "The Phillips doctrine thus amounts to institutionalizing Barry Goldwater's suggestion that the nation might be better off if its Northeastern corner were sawed off and allowed to drift out to sea." Warren Weaver, Jr., *New York Times* (September 21, 1969), BR3. The governor of Pennsylvania voiced similar concerns. [No author], "Governor Shafer Says He Fears G.O.P. Writes Off Northeast," *New York Times* (December 7, 1969), 60.
[23] Phillips, *Emerging Republican Majority*, 78.
[24] Ibid., 33.

The bold statement was that the clue to the future of the party was to focus on appealing to George Wallace's 1968 supporters:

> Although the Republican Party suffered a bad national defeat in 1964, the new ground broken aligned the GOP with a rising popular impetus, not a declining establishmentarian one.[25] Some of Wallace's support came from aroused conservative Republicans, but most of it represented Democratic streams quitting their party.[26] ... [A] relatively conservative 1968–1972 Republican administration should [result in adding] as an important national bloc of popular votes a key Deep Southern group of electoral votes to the barebones Republican triumph of 1968.[27] The big city political era is over. The GOP can build a winning coalition without Negro votes.[28]

Over the next four years, Richard Nixon attempted to act on the logic that there was a conservative base he could attract.[29] His challenge was to appeal to a diverse coalition of conservatives, all the while not going so far in that direction that he would alienate too much of the traditional Republican base. Nixon faced the task of preparing for another presidential campaign at a time when electoral bases were in transition. There was considerable ambiguity as to whether he could attract former Democrats fast enough to replace Republicans he might lose in the Northeast. Nixon appealed to anticommunist conservatives by maintaining the stance that he would not surrender to communists in Southeast Asia. He appealed to those supporting traditionalist norms and morals by continually expressing his support for law and order and his opposition to protesters and rioters. Vice-President Spiro Agnew played the role of creating "positive polarization" by articulating his dismissal of protesters and those who rejected traditional values. Nixon appealed to southerners worried about federal government intrusions to

[25] Ibid., 77.
[26] Ibid., 33.
[27] Ibid., 35.
[28] Ibid., 467–468.
[29] Perlstein, *Nixonland*, 459–525.

require desegregation by stressing that he would do only what the law required. In the 1972 campaign, he was fortunate that the Democrats nominated South Dakota Senator George McGovern, who was quickly labeled as a liberal and even a radical. The result was a resounding victory in 1972. Richard Nixon lost the presidency in 1960 and listened to the debate about whether he should have done more to appeal to the Northeast or pursue the South. He assessed the 1964 results and in 1968 sought to carefully capitalize on the strength Goldwater had shown in that race. From 1968 through 1972, he made the appeal more explicit and in the latter year won all of the southern states.

THE EFFECTS OF PARTY CHANGE
WITHIN THE NORTHEAST

From 1960 through 1972, the Republican Party underwent a significant change. Much of that change is reflected in its presidential candidates over that time. Candidates were listening to the diverse concerns being expressed by the voters and assessing their prospects for winning an election. The chronology of Republican candidates' stances indicates just how much change was occurring. When Richard Nixon ran in 1960, he sought to steer a middle course between two competing visions of the party and their respective candidates, Nelson Rockefeller and Barry Goldwater. Following Nixon's loss in 1960, the party image, at least as embodied in its presidential candidate, became much more conservative with the candidacy of Barry Goldwater and his pursuit of a Southern Strategy. Then in 1968, Richard Nixon moved the image somewhat back to the middle as he sought to continue the Southern Strategy while struggling to maneuver between George Wallace and Hubert Humphrey. In 1972, with Wallace removed from the race, Nixon was able to concentrate on trying to attract his supporters to create a new coalition. Across the decade, the party's presidential candidate moved from being mildly supportive of civil rights to growing opposition. The congressional Republican Party became less supportive of civil rights

TABLE 5.1. *Republican Presidential vote percentages by area of nation, 1900–72*

Years	Area of Nation		
	Northeast	South	Other
1900–28	56.0	26.3	51.0
1932–60	51.1	30.2	47.8
1964–72	44.5	51.7	50.0
Change, 1900–28 to 1964–72	−11.5	+25.4	−1.0
1960	48.5	43.9	52.7
1964	31.4	52.9	39.8
1968	43.7	32.3	48.8
1972	58.4	69.8	61.5
Change, 1960–72	+9.9	+25.9	+8.8

Source: Data compiled by authors. The percentages are averages of average yearly state percentages of the total vote, and not of the two-party vote. That is, the state percentages for, for example, 1900 are averaged, the same is done for the other years, and the yearly averages for 1900–28 are then averaged.

legislation.[30] The party was changing its positions. How did these transitions affect the party in the Northeast?

For decades, the northeastern states had been the most reliable Republican states. The rise of the conservative movement and the pursuit of the Southern Strategy was a direct message to the "liberal establishment" Northeast that there was going to be less responsiveness to their concerns. The result was a clear shift in the party's appeal by region. Table 5.1 indicates just how much change had occurred. In the 1900–28 elections, the party received its highest percentage in presidential elections in the Northeast. When the New Deal coalition dominated national politics from 1932 to 1960, the party still did best within the Northeast.

In the election of 1964 and those that followed, the geographical electoral success of the party shifted, with Republican

---

[30] Carmines and Stimson, *Issue Evolution*, 61–64.

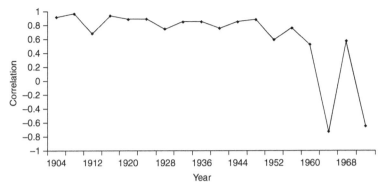

Figure 5.2. Correlation of Republican state Presidential percentages for 1904–72 with those for 1900.

presidential candidates improving their support in the South. In 1972, Richard Nixon did well all across the nation, but the important matter was that by that year, the Republican Party candidate received his highest percentage in the South. The dramatic nature of this shift can be seen in Figure 5.2. The graph presents the extent to which state results from later years correlate with those from 1900. For this graph, the state percentages for the years 1904, 1908, and so forth up through 1972 are correlated with the percentages of 1900. From 1904 through 1960, the party's relative success by state remained remarkably stable with what prevailed in 1900. Then the Goldwater candidacy abruptly and dramatically altered the party's relative success across states. The states where the party had done best in the past became the states where it now did worst. In 1968, it appeared that normalcy returned, but that was only because Wallace took so many votes that Nixon might have won. In 1972, Nixon essentially replicated the disjuncture in relative success that Goldwater had created; the correlation between their votes in 1964 and 1972 was +.70.

From 1968 to 1972, Richard Nixon set out to attract the vote of George Wallace and add it to the vote Nixon received in the three-way race of 1968. The correlation across states between Wallace's 1968 vote percentages and Goldwater's support in 1964 was .80. That is, their relative success across the states was very similar. The

TABLE 5.2. *Republican House candidates in the Northeast, 1900–72*

Years	% seats won in region	% of all seats from	% vote won in region
1900–28	72.8	38.3	52.8
1932–60	56.0	38.3	48.3
1964–72	43.4	25.8	44.5
Change	−29.4	−12.5	−8.3

Source. Data compiled by authors. The percentages are averages of average yearly district percentages of the total vote, and not of the two-party vote. That is, the district percentages within a year are averaged and those yearly district averages are then averaged for the years 1900–28.

correlation between Nixon's 1972 vote percentage and the Nixon *plus* Wallace percentage in 1968 was .81.[31] Nixon's 1972 vote had a correlation with the 1900 vote of −.64. Nixon did best where the party had done badly in the past and he did worst where the party had done well. As the correlation shows, within a short time, the relative success of party presidential candidates had abruptly shifted. Nixon had succeeded in attracting the Wallace vote and in doing so he had solidified the transition that Goldwater began. By 1972, the Northeast had been relegated to considerably less importance for Republican presidential candidates.

The change was even more evident with Electoral College votes. From 1900 to 1928, Republican presidential candidates derived an average of 36.3 percent of their Electoral College votes from the Northeast. From 1932 to 1960, an average of 43.2 percent came from the Northeast. For 1960–72, an average of 8.8 percent came from the Northeast. The reliance of the party's presidential candidates on the Northeast had diminished considerably.

Similar changes were occurring in the House, as shown in Table 5.2. From 1900 to 1928, Republicans won an average of 72.8 percent of all seats in the region, and 38.3 percent of all Republican House seats came from the region. For 1960–72, they won an

[31] Mark D. Brewer and Jeffrey M. Stonecash, "Changing the Political Dialogue and Political Alignments: George Wallace and His 1968 Presidential Campaign," presented at the 2009 Midwest Political Science Association, April.

average of only 44.5 percent of the vote and only 43.4 percent of seats within the region. Only 25.8 percent of all the party's seats within the House came from the Northeast. The trend away from the party was also evident in state legislative races. As indicated in Figures 1.5 and 1.6, the average percentage of state legislative seats held by Democrats within the Northeast increased from about 30 percent in the late 1940s to 60 percent by the early 1970s. The trends did not suggest that the future of the party in the region was positive.

SHIFTS IN VOTER ATTACHMENTS

The 1960s shifted political results in the Northeast for Republicans. For decades, the party had a fairly consistent advantage within the region in winning states and congressional seats. That advantage was lost by 1972. While the party was losing voting support, was it permanently losing supporters? The issue is whether the shifts in party composition and concerns during the 1960s had created a fundamental shift in party attachments. Voters do not generally change their identification with a party quickly. They form attachments and when a party is changing, they take some time to reassess their party identification.[32] Table 5.3 indicates the identification and partisan voting by party identification from 1952 to 1972 for those within the Northeast.

While the party, primarily at the presidential level, but to a lesser extent at the congressional level, was shifting its policy positions and the voters it was pursuing, it was not yet creating a decline in voter identification within the Northeast. In 1952, 42.6 percent identified with the Republican Party and in 1972, following considerable change, 42.6 percent identified with the party. While the region was moving to vote more Democratic, there was no change in party identification. Democrats, despite gains in votes, actually lost two percentage points in party identification over the twenty years.

The change in voting results was due to declines in party voting among party identifiers. Following the 1950s, Democrats became

---

[32] Jeffrey M. Stonecash, *Political Parties Matter: Realignment and the Return of Partisanship* (Boulder, CO: Lynne Rienner, 2006), 109–128.

TABLE 5.3. *Party identification within the Northeast and partisan voting*

Party ID	1952	1956	1958	1960	1962	1964	1966	1968	1970	1972
Democrat	50.6	52.0	48.3	45.0	50.8	54.4	53.3	48.4	48.4	48.7
Independent	6.8	8.6	6.4	8.9	5.6	8.0	6.1	9.8	7.0	8.8
Republican	42.6	39.4	45.3	46.1	43.6	37.6	40.6	41.8	44.6	42.6
Percent Voting for Democratic Presidential Candidate by Party ID										
Democrat	73.9	71.2		85.1		94.6		80.7		64.5
Independent	18.2	18.8		66.7		86.4		40.0		33.3
Republican	5.8	4.2		12.1		41.8		8.4		13.8
Percent Voting for Democratic House Candidates by Party ID										
Democrat	72.8	82.7	90.7	84.2	90.1	90.7	87.5	80.3	82.9	85.2
Independent	20.0	31.0	41.2	54.6	50.0	81.3	70.0	46.6	54.6	57.3
Republican	13.0	6.2	12.4	11.4	18.0	26.3	37.3	17.2	12.9	23.0

Source: NES Cumulative File, 1948–2004. Party identification is defined as those initially indicating a party identification plus those who initially indicated they are independent but said they identify with a party when asked if they lean toward either party. The percentages are taken from those who report voting in the presidential election. Respondents who did not report voting are excluded.

more supportive of their presidential candidates, except for 1972 when George McGovern lost badly. That also occurred in congressional elections. Over that time period, in contrast, the defection rate of Republican identifiers from their candidates increased. In the 1950s, the average percentage of Republican identifiers who voted Democratic was 5.0 in presidential elections and 10.5 in House elections. After that, the average increased to 19.1 percent in presidential elections and 20.7 percent in House elections. Voters were not yet shifting their party identification away from the Republican Party, but they were less willing to support it in elections.

The 1964 election was particularly significant. As Figure 1.1 in Chapter 1 indicates, 1960 was the first time since 1928 that Democrats won a higher percentage of the presidential vote in the Northeast than elsewhere (52.6 percent to 48.5 percent). Then in 1964, they achieved their highest-ever percentage in the Northeast (68.5) and held an advantage over the rest of the nation of a varying magnitude in every year thereafter. What was causing the party problems in 1964? More specifically, what was the problem that Republicans in the Northeast had with the party in that election? Was there a pattern to whom they lost in that election? Table 5.4 provides evidence about that.

In the 1964 election, Goldwater was arguing that the federal government was becoming too powerful and that civil rights legislation was unnecessary. At a time when a great moral dilemma was being presented to the American public, Goldwater was saying that the federal government in general should not intrude into state affairs and particularly on this issue. In making this appeal, he was advocating positions that were least likely to be well received in the Northeast. As the table shows, in 1964, Northeast Republicans were most supportive of a Negro's (as phrased in that year's question) right to have the same access to housing as others. Goldwater was appealing to the South, which was least supportive of that right. In making his argument about the federal government, he was also facing the fact that the Northeast was least

TABLE 5.4. *Opinions about federal power and racial integration by region, all respondents*[33]

Questions	Northeast	South	Other
Housing Integration			
Whites have right to exclude	14.3	61.8	26.1
Negroes have right to housing	85.7	38.2	73.9
Power of Federal Government			
Has gotten too powerful	58.2	75.0	73.1
Depends	2.2	0.0	3.9
Has not gotten too powerful	39.6	25.0	23.1

likely to agree with his position. His positions clashed with the Northeast more than elsewhere.[34]

Not only were northeastern Republicans more liberal than Republicans in the rest of the country (as the conservatives always argued), but those with liberal opinions on these issues were much more likely to defect to Lyndon Johnson in the presidential race. Table 5.5 indicates how those Republicans with different opinions on federal power and housing integration voted in the

---

[33] Results taken from the NES 1964 survey.
[34] In focusing on these two issues, it is not presumed that race and federal power to address this issue were the only issues the Republican Party was emphasizing or that these two issues dominated others within this time period. The predominant images that voters had of the parties and which issues were most influential in shaping voter choices over time are a disputed matter and beyond the scope of this book. This matter of ambiguity is particularly important in assessing the impact of the Southern Strategy. There are some who assert that "race and ethnicity overshadow economic class …" Earl Black and Merle Black, *The Rise of Southern Republicans* (Cambridge: Harvard University Press, 2002), 246. In this view, race is central to the image the party was presenting. Despite those claims, there is an equally plausible narrative that Republicans were appealing to individualism and limited government, and that the dominant response in the South was the opening of a significant class division where none had existed before. For evidence of that, see Mark D. Brewer and Jeffrey M. Stonecash, "Class, Race Issues, and Declining White Support for the Democratic Party in the South," *Political Behavior*, 23, no. 2 (June 2001), 131–156. We use these issues to illustrate the problems Republicans encountered in the Northeast and not as the defining issues in that year or the decade.

TABLE 5.5. *Opinions about federal power and racial integration and vote in 1964 Presidential election, Republicans only, by region*

	Johnson	Goldwater	Other
Outside the Northeast			
All	21.3	78.0	.7
Housing Integration			
Whites have right to exclude	20.6	79.5	0
Negroes have right to housing	24.0	74.7	1.3
Power of Federal Government			
Has gotten too powerful	11.5	87.9	.6
Has not gotten too powerful	37.8	62.2	0
Northeast			
All	41.4	57.7	1.0
Housing Integration			
Whites have right to exclude	20.0	80.0	0
Negroes have right to housing	48.1	50.7	1.3
Power of Federal Government			
Has gotten too powerful	19.6	78.3	2.2
Has not gotten too powerful	58.1	41.9	0

Source: The 1964 NES study.

1964 election. Outside the Northeast, 21.3 percent of Republicans defected to vote for Lyndon Johnson. Opinions about housing integration had a modest effect on creating defections, whereas opinions about federal power had a greater effect. Among those who did not think the federal government had gotten too powerful, 37.8 percent defected to Lyndon Johnson.

Within the Northeast, 41.4 percent of all Republicans defected to Johnson. Those within the Northeast were more liberal about both of these issues and more likely to defect when they held a liberal position. Among those liberal about housing integration, 48.1 percent defected. Among those who thought the government

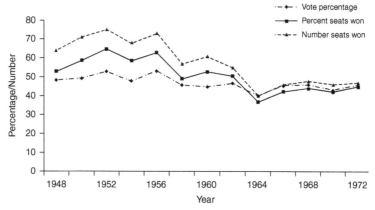

Figure 5.3. Success of House Republicans in the Northeast, 1948–72.

was not too powerful, 58.1 percent defected. The message that
Goldwater presented was not well received within the nation and
pushed many Republicans to vote for Johnson – especially in the
Northeast.

Richard Nixon was able to help bring back Republican support
in the Northeast in 1968 and 1972, getting over 50 percent within
the region in each election and winning four of the ten states in
1968 and nine of ten in 1972. The party, however, did not recover
from the damage of the Goldwater campaign in House elections.
Figure 5.3 indicates how Republican House candidates fared in
the Northeast from 1948 through 1972. The party's situation
had not been strong to begin with. From 1948 through 1956, its
average percentage in the Northeast hovered around 50 percent.
Despite this closeness, the party often won 60 percent of all seats.
Then the 1958 election brought their vote percentage below 50,
and their percentage of seats down to 50. Their results stabilized
at those levels through 1962. Then the 1964 election lowered their
average percentage to 40.0 and their percentage of seats to 36.7.
This created many Democratic incumbents who held onto office
in subsequent years. The effect of the Goldwater campaign in the
Northeast proved to be enduring.

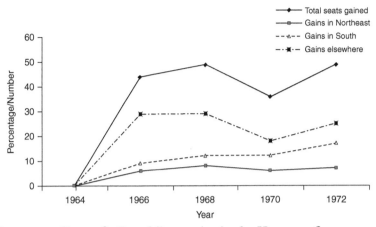

Figure 5.4. Post-1964 Republican gains in the House, 1964–72.

The results of subsequent elections in the Northeast and elsewhere pushed along the declining relevance of the Northeast for
the party. The 1964 election was a low point for the party, which
soon bounced back nationally. It was where the party regained
seats that created more problems for northeastern Republicans.
Figure 5.4 tracks the total gains made by the party from its low
point in 1964. Following the 1964 elections, the party held 147
seats in the House. While some party members surely sought to
regain seats in areas the party held prior to 1964, others were
looking for where the party gained as a sign of the future. From
the 147 held after the 1964 elections, the party increased its total
number in 1966 to 191 and in subsequent years they held 196
(1968), 183 (1970), and 196 (1972) seats.

The important matter was where the party realized gains. In
1962, Republicans held 55 seats in the Northeast. They lost 15
seats in the 1964 elections in the Northeast. With the resulting
40 as a base, in subsequent elections the net gains relative to the
40 was 6 to reach 46 in 1966, 8 to 48 in 1968, 6 to 46 in 1970, and
7 to 47 in 1972. The gains from 1964 to 1972 in the Northeast
were limited. In contrast, in the South, the gains in seats were
cumulative gains of 9, then 12, then 12 again, and then a net

increase of 17 by 1972. Their fortunes were steadily improving there. Elsewhere in the country, the party experienced even bigger gains, gaining relative to 1964 29, 29, 18, and 25 seats in those years respectively. The prospects for the future in the Northeast did not look good.

A DECADE OF TRANSITION

When the 1960s began, the Republican Party was doing well within the Northeast, having won most states in the 1950s in presidential elections and a majority of House seats. Tensions existed between the conservative and moderate-liberal factions within the party, but they had not yet become a full-blown contest. The frustrations of conservatives eventually prompted them to target the South and nominate a conservative presidential candidate. They succeeded and changed the national image of the party, with Goldwater forcefully opposing a significant role for the federal government and in particular the historic 1964 Civil Rights Act. The election created major losses for the party and a major shift in where the party did well. The election fundamentally altered the relative success of the party across states. Republicans appeared to bounce back in presidential elections in 1968 and 1972, winning those contests and largely regaining their previous number of seats in the House. By 1972, the party was winning fewer House seats in the Northeast than it had in 1962 and in presidential elections was now doing better outside the Northeast than within it. The conservative wing of the party was now dominant, the pursuit of the Southern Strategy continued, and the Northeast had been relegated to lesser relevance within the party. The shift to a conservative image had significant consequences for the northeastern wing of the party.

CHAPTER 6

Social Change, Party Response, and Further Republican Losses

As the 1970s began, the situation of the national Republican Party was decidedly mixed. Richard Nixon won re-election by a large margin in 1972, giving the party two presidents winning consecutive terms within twenty years. In that election, the party gained 12 seats in the House, bringing their total to 192. In the Senate, the party won 17 of the 33 seats up for election. Despite this good news, the difficulties the party faced were significant. It was in the minority in each house of Congress. The percentage of respondents identifying with the Republican Party was not increasing. The party image presented by Nixon was muddled. On the one hand, he proposed the guaranteed income tax; on the other hand, he made it clear that he would not be aggressive in pursuing civil rights cases or busing. In the 1972 campaign, he pursued Wallace voters and created an electoral coalition comprised of his 1968 vote plus many of Wallace's supporters. The party was making gains in winning congressional seats in the South but not fast enough to become solidly conservative and rely on southern seats.

For the Northeast, Nixon's position of expressing sympathy for the South and pursuing a southern strategy created problems because many in the Northeast were uncomfortable with policies that supported resistance to civil rights. While Nixon did well in the Northeast in 1972, his support did not translate into greater support for House candidates. Republican House candidates were receiving less than 50 percent of the vote (Figure 5.3) and winning less than 50 percent of seats.

The party's situation quickly changed nationally and within the Northeast. In 1973 and 1974, the Watergate scandal unfolded, with the White House eventually ensnared in the attempt to cover up the break-in at the Democratic national headquarters. As the scandal developed, the result was that many voters saw it as a Republican Party scandal. Richard Nixon was forced to resign in August 1974, three months before the off-year elections. The subsequent elections produced a resounding defeat for the party. Republicans lost 49 seats in the House, giving Democrats a 292–143 advantage. In the Senate elections, Democrats won 23 of 34 contests, giving them a 60–38 advantage.

Within the Northeast, the election had a particularly damaging impact. In 1970, the party won 46 of 109 House seats and in 1972 it won 47 of 105. In the 1974 elections, Republicans won only 34 of 105 House seats, for 32.4 percent of seats. Things did not get better in subsequent years. In an effort to avoid a lengthy prosecution of an ex-president, Nixon's successor, Gerald Ford, decided to put the issue in the past and pardoned Nixon. His job approval ratings immediately dropped and he narrowly lost the 1976 presidential election. In 1976, the party lost another House seat in the Northeast, dropping to 33. Then in 1978, they lost another one. Each election of 1974, 1976, and 1978 produced new historic lows in terms of the percentage of seats held in the Northeast, ending with 30.5 percent of seats in 1978.

The issue the party faced, with Goldwater, Nixon, and Watergate in the past, was whether it could make a comeback in the Northeast. The concern was which way the party would go. The 1970s were a decade in which it was difficult for many to see a clear direction for either party. To many observers it appeared to be a decade in which parties were becoming less relevant. Nationally more voters were saying that they did not identify with a party and more were engaging in ticket-splitting. The differences between parties in Congress were at a low point. In House districts, the percentage of cases in which the winner of the House election and the presidential election differed was steadily increasing.[1] It was an era in

---

[1]   Stonecash, *Political Parties Matter*, 68.

which many saw parties as declining in relevance[2] and Members of Congress as operating independently of parties.[3] Yet the decade was really transitional for parties. Each was losing its former solid base. For Democrats, the South was no longer invariably theirs. Republicans had lost dominance in the Northeast and had to decide whether to make any efforts to try to regain support within the region.

Three matters played a major role in the Republican's decision. First, the distribution of regional strength within the party was continuing to shift. Second, this was contributing to a further shift in the relative role of old and new conservative principles within the party. Third, the society was also changing and those changes played out very differently across the regions of America. The changes affected what each region wanted from government and which party philosophy was most compatible with the region. The result was that the concerns of the Northeast became less and less compatible with the philosophy of the Republican Party. The impact of these trends took a while to occur, but eventually they further eroded Republican support within the Northeast.

THE CHANGING BASE OF THE REPUBLICAN PARTY

Presidential candidate calculations are again important in driving change. Candidates must assess the political terrain and focus on the areas where they can win votes. The first challenge of any candidate is to win the party nomination, and the calculations for this were steadily shifting. The rules for allocating convention delegates awarded votes on the basis of the prior performance of a state in the presidential election.[4] Because Eisenhower had done relatively well in 1952 and 1956 in the South, that increased the allocation to

[2] David Broder, *The Party's Over: The Failure of Politics in America* (New York: Harper & Row, 1972); and William Crotty, *American Political Parties in Decline*, 2nd Ed. (Boston: Little, Brown, 1984).

[3] David Mayhew, *The Electoral Connection* (New Haven, CT: Yale University Press, 1974).

[4] Rae, *The Decline and Fall of Liberal Republicans*, 56.

that region. In 1964, Goldwater did even better in the South and in 1972 Nixon won all the southern states. Over this time, the population growth in the South and the West was much greater than in the Northeast and Midwest, further increasing the presidential votes recorded in these regions and the percentage of convention delegates awarded to the South and the West. The result was that the South was steadily increasing its percentage of all convention delegates and by 1976, the South, by a small margin, had the highest percentage of delegates at the nominating convention. Together the South and West had 47 percent of all delegates.[5]

The conservatives in these regions were different from those elsewhere, and they provided the basis for a different appeal. The South and West were growing and populated by many private sector entrepreneurs who were individualistic and did not see themselves as needing government.[6] These regions, and particularly the South, also contained more social conservatives troubled by trends in moral behavior in the nation. They were particularly troubled by protests, crime, greater reliance on government welfare, use of abortion, and illegitimate births.[7] Candidates like Barry Goldwater and Ronald Reagan appealed to these voters by emphasizing their opposition to the growth of government programs and their support for traditional morals.

The shifting position of the party is evident in the success of Ronald Reagan within his party over time. He first became prominent because of his support for the candidacy of Barry Goldwater. In 1966, Reagan surprised many by making a run for governor of California against a sitting Democrat, Pat Brown. He stressed themes of limited government and opposition to social disorder and protests, and won. In 1968, with no incumbent Republican president, Reagan contended for but lost the party nomination. Despite losing he was becoming the representative of arguments

[5] Ibid., 117.
[6] Lisa McGirr, *Suburban Warriors* (Princeton, NJ: Princeton University Press, 2002); and Matthew D. Lassiter, *The Silent Majority* (Princeton, NJ: Princeton University Press, 2006).
[7] Brewer and Stonecash, *Split*, Chapter 5.

TABLE 6.1. *Republican candidate nominating support by region, 1968 and 1976*

Region[8]	1968 Nomination			1976 Nomination	
	Nixon	Others[9]	Reagan	Ford	Reagan
Northeast	31.8	67.9	0.3	88.0	12.0
Midwest	52.6	44.6	2.8	68.0	32.0
South	74.2	7.6	18.2	18.0	82.0
West	47.7	11.8	40.4	27.0	73.0

Note: Percentages sum across within each year.

against a greater role for government and for supporting traditional morals within the party. In 1976, Reagan chose to oppose the nomination of a sitting Republican president, Gerald Ford, and nearly succeeded. Finally in 1980, running against George H. W. Bush, widely seen as an eastern candidate, Reagan succeeded in securing the nomination. When asked how he had changed to win the nomination, he replied "I have often thought the party changed more than I did."[10]

The important matter was where his brand of conservatism succeeded and what it suggested for the role of the Northeast within the party. The 1968 and 1976 contests are important as indicators of how a new conservative base within the party was emerging. Goldwater had secured the nomination by capitalizing on support within the West and South. Reagan drew upon that same base, as Table 6.1 indicates. In 1968, Reagan received 40.4 percent of the votes cast by western delegates and 18.2 percent of the southern votes. He probably would have done better in those areas if Nixon

[8] In this book, we define the South as the eleven former Confederate states. Because Delaware, Kentucky, Maryland, West Virginia, and the District of Columbia are not in other regions, and we are focusing on our narrow definition of the Northeast, we have allocated these states to the Midwest.

[9] These votes were for Nelson Rockefeller and Others. The results are taken from Rae, *The Decline and Fall of Liberal Republicans*, 98 and 117.

[10] Reported in "Franklin Delano Reagan," *New York Times* (July 20, 1980), E20. The response was to a question asked in a Bill Moyers interview earlier in the year.

had not devoted so much attention to them. Reagan received very few votes elsewhere. In 1976, running against a sitting president, Reagan did even better in the West and the South. He drew 73 percent of the western votes and 82 percent of the southern votes. He received little support within the Northeast.

While Nixon had sought the South in a low-key way while trying to retain support elsewhere in the nation, Reagan made a more direct appeal. In 1980, after securing the Republican nomination, he opened his general election campaign in Philadelphia, Mississippi, where three civil rights workers were murdered in 1964. Reagan stated, "Programs like education and others should be turned back to the states and local communities with the tax sources to fund them. I believe in states' right[s]. I believe in people doing as much as they can at the community level and the private level." He also stated, "I believe we have distorted the balance of our government today by giving powers that were never intended to be given in the Constitution to that federal establishment." He went on to promise to "restore to states and local governments the power that properly belongs to them."[11] It was hard to miss the message. He began his campaign in the South and made a strong statement in support of states' rights. Given the history of racial discrimination sanctioned by state law in the South and enforced by police authority, the appeal was clear. The conflict with the Northeast's relatively great support for civil rights was also clear. That conflict will be discussed further in this chapter.

Reagan was able to use that appeal to average 50 percent in southern states, despite running against a southern candidate, Jimmy Carter. He did well in the West and won the presidency. In 1984, he did better in all regions of the country, winning re-election in a landslide. In 1988, George H. W. Bush, his Vice-President, won all regions, beating Michael Dukakis.

The important matter for the Northeast was how the base of Republican presidential candidates had shifted. Table 6.2 presents

---

[11] Douglas E. Kneeland, "Reagan Campaigns at Mississippi Fair; Nominee Tells Crowd of 10,000 He Is Backing States' Rights," *New York Times* (August 4, 1980), A11.

TABLE 6.2. *Republican candidate general election support, by region, 1948–88*

Year	Northeast	Midwest	South	West
1948	50.2	46.9	23.6	46.0
1952	57.6	55.6	46.3	60.3
1956	62.8	58.2	44.8	58.4
1960	48.6	50.2	43.9	53.7
1964	31.4	36.8	52.9	40.9
1968	43.7	44.5	32.3	50.5
1972	58.4	58.9	69.8	62.5
1976	48.7	47.8	43.6	52.5
1980	47.1	48.3	50.0	57.6
1984	57.8	55.9	61.5	63.5
1988	52.0	51.4	58.3	54.9
Average margin of victory over Democrats				
1948 – 56	14.8	8.0	−9.8	11.0
1960 – 76	−5.7	−2.1	7.1	7.0
1980 – 88	9.2	6.9	14.9	21.2

the vote percentages won by Republican candidates from 1948 to 1988. For the years 1948–56, the party had its largest margin of victory in the Northeast. For the years 1960–76, the party had negative margins (lost) in the Northeast and Midwest. In the 1980–88 elections, the party did better everywhere, but its largest margins of victory were in the South and West.

While Republican presidential candidates were targeting the South and making the Northeast secondary in campaign plans, the congressional base was also shifting, but not so clearly. Congressional results generally lag presidential results and that was occurring again. Figure 6.1 indicates the percent of House seats won within regions of the nation from 1900 to 1988. Three matters are important. Over the years, the party had experienced a steady decline in its fortunes outside the South. The declines were both

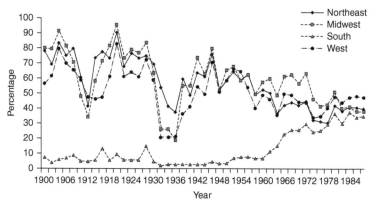

Figure 6.1. Percentage of House seats won by Republicans within regions, 1900–88.

abrupt (1932–36) and gradual (the early 1950s and afterward). The party recovered somewhat from the 1930s during the 1940s, but the long-term pattern was of declining support outside the South.

Second, the Northeast had experienced the greatest erosion. In the early 1900s, the party regularly won 80 percent of seats within the region. By 1980, it was winning 42 percent of all seats within the region. Perhaps most important for Ronald Reagan and his followers, Republican candidates were finally doing as well within the South as in other areas of the nation. While moderates within the party could look at the results and see declines across much of the country, the conservatives within the party saw good news: They were improving their situation in the most conservative region of the nation. Yet conservatives were also frustrated. The party had reached almost 40 percent of seats in the South by 1980 and was essentially stuck there. Further, in no region of the country was the party winning 50 percent of the seats. Some saw a strong need to establish a more distinct party identity.

THE CHANGING NORTHEAST
AND REPUBLICAN PHILOSOPHY

The 1980s represent a decade in which the Republican Party might have been seen as a national, though still minority, party.

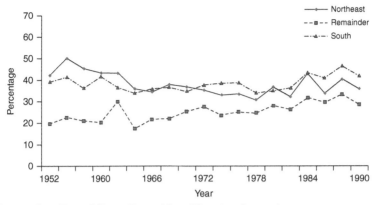

Figure 6.2. Republican Party identification by region, 1952–90.

As Table 6.2 indicates, Presidents Ronald Reagan and George H. W. Bush did fairly well across the regions of the nation. In House elections (Figure 6.1), the party's success by region was now uniform. The party might have sought to regain some of its support within the Northeast. As Figure 6.2 indicates, during the 1980s, identification with the Republican Party was still relatively good in the Northeast. Identification with the party within the region clearly slipped during the 1960s and 1970s, but during the 1980s it stabilized and reached 40 percent in 1984 and 1988.

Political support for Republicans in the Northeast seemed very similar to the rest of the nation. Its identification with the party was similar, and it was voting for Republicans at the same rate as other regions. When voters were asked if they saw themselves as liberal, moderate, or conservative, the percentage choosing conservative was very similar in the Northeast to the remainder of the nation. Within the nation in 1980, 28.3 percent defined themselves as conservative and within the Northeast, 27.5 percent did so. In 1984, the national percentage was 28.6; within the Northeast, it was 28.7. In 1992, the national percentage was 30.2 and within the Northeast it was 28.8. In many ways, the Northeast was not different from the nation.

Whereas the Northeast's partisanship looked much like the rest of the nation, its interests were changing and going in a different direction from that of the Republican Party. The conflict hurt

the party within the Northeast over the next several decades. The
Republican Party was becoming more conservative, and President
Reagan embodied that change with his articulate belief that government was not a solution to problems, but generally part of the
problem. He advocated lower taxes and less government activism
to provide programs and regulate private sector activity, and had
considerable faith in private markets.

Changes were occurring within the Northeast that made his
message less appealing within that region. The Northeast was
attracting a population that needed more government assistance
at the same time as the economy of the region was no longer growing as it once had. There had been a steady migration of blacks
from the South to the North in search of jobs.[12] Many blacks came
from an agricultural background in the South and lacked industrial skills. The presence of a wide array of factories in the North
that could employ those with modest skills provided many with
expanded opportunities. But many also lived in relative poverty in
northern cities. During this time, the Northeast began to slip as
a region experiencing growth. For decades it had been the most
economically developed and prosperous region of the nation,
with a per capita income that was considerably higher than that
of other regions.[13] It had a higher concentration of private and
public unions that secured higher wages for their members, and it
provided more generous public assistance benefits.[14]

This relative prosperity began to slip, with more and more of
the nation's population growth occurring outside the Northeast.
As Table 6.3 indicates, population growth within the Northeast
was limited while the South and West were growing rapidly. The
population of the South grew by 141.9 percent from 1950 to 2004,
while the average state grew 134.4 percent. Growth in the West was

[12] Nicholas Lemann, *The Promised Land: The Great Migration and How it Changed America* (New York: Knopf, 1991).

[13] Advisory Commission on Intergovernmental Relations, *Regional Growth: Historic Perspective* (Washington, DC: U.S. Government Printing Office, 1980).

[14] Mark Rom, "Health and Welfare in the American States: Politics and Policies," in Virginia Gray and Herbert Jacob, eds., *Politics in the American States: A Comparative Analysis*, 6th Ed. (Washington, DC: CQ Press, 1996), p. 415.

TABLE 6.3. *Population change by region, 1950–2004*

Region	Total Population (In thousands)			Average %
	1950	2004	% increase	State Increase
Northeast	39,478	54,572	38.2	58.7
Midwest	38,049	59,337	55.9	69.7
South	37,587	90,911	141.9	134.4
West	35,414	88,284	149.3	205.7

Source: U.S. Statistical Abstract.

even greater. The greater growth in these regions created a sense of prosperity and less of a sense of needing government than in other regions of the nation.[15] In the Northeast, there was anxiety about a lack of growth and its impact on jobs.

The relative lack of population growth in the Northeast was accompanied by a decline in manufacturing and union membership. The entire nation was losing manufacturing jobs, because many companies pursued cheap labor elsewhere in the world, but the biggest losses were in the Northeast. As the population grew elsewhere, many older firms chose to close up factories with older equipment in the Northeast and establish newer ones in the South and West where markets were growing and labor costs were often cheaper. Many new firms also chose to start up in the South and West. As Table 6.4 indicates, the result was a relatively greater decline in manufacturing jobs after the 1950s in the Northeast. In 1950, 35 percent of jobs within the Northeast were in manufacturing; by 2004, 9.1 percent were. Many of the lost jobs had been relatively well-paying jobs with pensions and health insurance.

As manufacturing and union jobs declined, there was considerable concern within many northeastern states about the future of jobs in the region and about tax bases to support the high level of services that were common in these states. There was support

---

[15] McGirr, *Suburban Warriors*; Lassiter, *The Silent Majority*.

TABLE 6.4. *Manufacturing employment by region, 1950–2004*

Region	Percent Employment in Manufacturing			Average %
	1950	2004	% Change	State Change
Northeast	35.0	9.1	−25.9	−27.1
Midwest	33.5	13.4	−20.1	−18.3
South	18.4	9.9	−8.5	−7.3
West	16.1	9.2	6.9	−3.2

for using government to help attract new businesses and jobs and to help retrain workers who had lost jobs. The combination of eroding jobs and the migration of poor blacks into the North also created a greater need for public welfare. The North had long had higher welfare payments and made access to obtaining welfare easier.

These changes were altering the region's position on free trade and the relative attractiveness of the Republican and Democratic parties to voters in the Northeast. During the 1940s and 1950s, Democrats had been supportive of reduced restrictions on international trade and Republicans had supported some restrictions to protect industry. As the Republican base shifted to the West and South where growth was occurring, the party saw less need for restrictions and protection. Democrats were making gains in the North and were supportive of trade restrictions to protect industries in the North. During the 1960s, the parties switched positions on trade issues and Democrats, and particularly those in the North, became opponents of reducing trade restrictions.[16] Their argument was that they needed to protect industries and jobs that contributed to better standards of living for workers. At a time when Ronald Reagan and the Republicans were advocating less government and arguing that international trade

[16] Nicole Mellow, *The State of Disunion: Regional Sources of Modern American Partisanship* (Baltimore: Johns Hopkins University Press, 2008), 46–81; David Karol, *Party Position Change in American Politics* (New York: Cambridge University Press, 2009).

would produce cheaper goods for Americans, many communities in the Northeast were worried about retaining jobs and were represented by Democrats who were opposing free trade legislation. Further, Democrats were proposing programs to help communities and manufacturing workers make transitions to a different economy. The Republican messages that government action was detrimental and that welfare should be cut were not likely to be well received in communities in the Northeast that were experiencing job losses and where there was considerable poverty in cities.[17]

The shift to a more conservative Republican Party had a particularly negative impact on the northeastern wing of the party for several reasons. The Northeast as a whole had more liberals and moderates than the rest of the nation, and Northeast Republicans were not as conservative as the rest of the party. Since 1972, the National Election Studies have been asking people to place themselves ideologically. Respondents were asked if they regarded themselves as conservative, moderate, liberal, or haven't thought much about it.

In using these responses, it is important to note that what respondents mean by liberal, moderate, or conservative when they place themselves is subjective and by no means clear. Respondents are not given a definition of the terms, so each individual defines that on his or her own, making it difficult to be certain about the content individuals have in mind. Further, the content of being liberal, moderate, or conservative may change over time. The ideas of social conservatives, to be discussed shortly, were not a clear part of ideological differences in the 1960s and 1970s, but have gradually become more important.[18] In the 1960s, most conservative Republicans probably thought primarily in terms of limited government. Over time, more have come to incorporate notions of preserving traditional values, changing the content of conservatism.[19]

[17] Mellow, *The State of Disunion*, 82–132.
[18] For example, see Critchlow, *The Conservative Ascendancy*.
[19] Marc J. Hetherington and Jonathan D. Weiler, *Authoritarianism and Polarization in American Politics* (New York: Cambridge University Press, 2009);

Nonetheless, the differences by region and the changing distributions over time are important.

Table 6.5 addresses the overall distribution of responses by
region and decade. The responses are grouped by decade to
focus on broad changes over time and not on year-to-year fluctuations. Over time, the long-term polarization of parties around
ideology is affecting voters and more of them are choosing sides.[20]
The percentage of respondents who decline to place themselves
has decreased in all regions. Most important, the Northeast
has consistently had a higher percentage of respondents who
regard themselves as liberal or moderate. The South, the region
Republicans were pursuing, has the lowest percentage of liberals
and moderates. The Republican Party nationally was moving to
a more conservative position while the Northeast as a region has
had a higher percentage of liberals and moderates.

This greater presence of liberals and moderates within the
Northeast affected the composition of the Republican Party
in the 1970s. Table 6.6 indicates two important features of
northeastern Republicans: their ideological composition over
time and the defection rates by ideological position. The composition of the party is shown to the left. In the 1970s, among
Republicans in the Northeast, 47 percent defined themselves as
conservative, a somewhat smaller percentage of the party than
elsewhere. The interesting matters are how defection rates differed by region and what happened after the 1970s to liberals
and moderates among northeastern Republicans. A party defec-
tor can be defined as someone who identifies with the party but
then votes for a candidate who is not a Republican. The right
side of the table indicates the percentage of those who say they
are liberal-moderate, undefined, or conservative and then
vote for a non-Republican presidential candidate. Self-defined

[20] Alan I. Abramowitz and Kyle L. Saunders, "Ideological Realignments in the U.S.
Electorate," *Journal of Politics* 60 (August 1998), 634–652; and Kyle L. Saunders
and Alan I. Abramowitz, "The Rise of the Ideological Voter: The Changing Bases of
Partisanship in the American Electorate," in John C. Green and Daniel J. Coffey, eds.,
The State of the Parties, 5th Ed. (New York: Rowman and Littlefield, 2007), 299–315.

TABLE 6.5. *Ideological identification by region, 1970s–2000s*

Decade	Ideology											
	Liberal + Moderate			Conservative			None		
	NE	South	Remainder	NE	South	Remainder	NE	South	Remainder
1970s	50.1	36.4	47.1	24.7	25.3	28.4	25.1	38.3	24.5
1980s	45.0	33.9	41.6	26.8	27.0	31.3	28.3	39.1	27.1
1990s	49.3	34.8	45.8	29.1	28.9	33.1	21.6	36.3	21.1
2000s	53.4	38.8	48.4	32.5	37.6	33.8	14.1	23.7	17.8

Note: None consists of those who say they had not thought of the matter or who offered no response.
Source: NES cumulative file, 1948–2004 and 2008 study. For the 2000s, the results are the average of the years 2000, 2002, 2004, and 2008.

TABLE 6.6. *Ideological placement among Republicans and defections in Presidential elections by ideology, 1970s–2000s*

Decade	Ideological Placement			Defection Percentage		
	Lib-mod	None	Cons	Lib-mod	None	Cons
1970s						
Northeast	34.9	17.9	47.2	20.5	26.7	5.9
South	27.6	21.9	50.5	9.3	11.6	10.1
Remainder	35.5	14.1	50.4	13.6	18.8	4.7
1980s						
Northeast	29.4	19.0	51.6	19.8	11.9	7.5
South	21.5	17.8	60.8	11.3	7.8	3.4
Remainder	25.1	18.2	56.7	15.7	12.4	7.3
1990s						
Northeast	29.5	12.1	58.4	47.1	33.3	27.7
South	24.2	8.3	67.5	34.5	25.0	16.1
Remainder	25.2	11.0	63.8	40.5	38.3	18.4
2000s						
Northeast	25.5	2.0	72.5	32.0	50.0	2.8
South	21.6	14.2	64.2	8.6	13.0	1.9
Remainder	27.8	8.5	63.8	22.5	3.7	8.9

conservatives defect at low rates, while liberals and moderates defect at higher rates. In the Northeast, liberals-moderates have consistently defected in presidential voting at higher rates than liberal-moderate Republicans elsewhere. Northeastern liberal-moderate Republicans apparently experienced more ideological conflict with their party and defected.

That conflict eventually had an effect on the inclination of Republican liberals and moderates in the Northeast to stay within the party. Over the next three decades, the percent of party identifiers who were liberal or moderate declined, as did those with no placement. The result was a significant increase of Republican identifiers within the Northeast indicating that they were conservative, paralleling a pattern occurring across the nation.[21] Those who were not conservative were leaving the party. This sorting out was greater in the Northeast. From the 1970s through the 2000s, conservatives came to comprise a greater percentage of northeastern Republicans because liberals and moderates left the party. By the 2000s, conservatives comprised 72.5 percent of Republican identifiers, whereas in other regions conservatives comprised roughly 64 percent of Republican identifiers.

The shift in the composition of the Republican Party was because the electorate was gradually realigning, or sorting itself out.[22] As Table 6.7 indicates, over time, liberals and moderates who were once Republican were increasingly identifying with the Democratic Party whereas conservatives were choosing the Republican Party.[23] This was happening in all regions. The percentage choosing Independent was also declining. The shift of liberals and moderates to the Democratic Party was particularly strong within the Northeast. Liberals and moderates were less likely to identify with the Democratic Party in the 1970s but by the 2000s, their identification as Democratic was higher than elsewhere in the nation. Not only did the Northeast have a higher percentage of liberals and moderates, but they identified with the Democratic Party at a higher rate than elsewhere in the nation. Again, while how respondents understand these terms is not known, it appears that the pursuit of a more conservative, antigovernment stance has registered with voters and prompted more and more liberals and moderates within the Northeast to move to the Democratic Party. The Republican strategy of trying to attract

[21] Jeffrey M. Stonecash, "The Rise of the Right: More Conservatives or More Concentrated Conservativism?" in John C. Green and Daniel J. Coffey, eds., *The State of the Parties*, 5th Ed. (New York: Rowman and Littlefield, 2007), 317–327.

[22] Morris P. Fiorina, *Cultural War?* (New York: Pearson/Longman, 2005).

[23] A survey of 400 Republicans in Pennsylvania in 2008, who had left the party in 2006 and 2007, supports this. Those Republicans who defected from the party were much more likely to define themselves as liberal (27 percent) or moderate (37 percent). See Chris Borick, "Where Have all the Republicans Gone? An Examination of the Causes of the Demise of Republican Party Registration," presented at the 2009 Annual Meeting of the American Association of Public Opinion Research, May.

TABLE 6.7. *Party identification by ideological placement, by region, 1970s–2000s*

Decade	Region								
	Northeast			South			Remainder		
	R	I	D	R	I	D	R	I	D
Liberals-moderates									
1970s	23.8	16.0	60.2	19.7	12.9	67.4	27.0	12.7	60.3
1980s	25.1	10.6	64.3	23.8	11.0	65.2	27.9	9.7	62.4
1990s	24.0	12.2	63.8	24.2	12.8	63.0	26.3	7.5	66.2
2000s	20.3	8.1	71.7	28.8	8.5	62.7	23.3	7.6	69.1
Conservatives									
1970s	59.7	8.8	31.6	42.8	11.1	46.3	64.3	9.7	26.0
1980s	63.6	8.9	27.5	51.9	9.3	38.9	67.2	7.3	25.4
1990s	60.7	9.3	30.0	61.9	4.6	33.6	71.1	6.5	22.5
2000s	74.5	6.1	19.4	74.4	4.1	21.5	79.0	4.9	16.1

conservatives was working all across the nation, but it was driving away liberals and moderates that constituted a substantial percentage of the Northeast. Creating a clear identity was winning and losing voters.

ANOTHER JUNCTURE: MINORITY STATUS AND PURSUING SOCIAL CONSERVATIVES

By the early 1990s, the Republican Party had made some gains. The party held the presidency for twelve consecutive years. It was making gains in party identification in the South and had stabilized its levels of support elsewhere in the nation (Figure 6.2). However, it lost the 1992 presidential election and remained in the minority in the House of Representatives, as it had been since 1954. The percentage of voters identifying with the Republicans was consistently less than that identifying with the Democrats. The party still faced the issue of how to become the majority party.

They needed to find another constituency to expand their electoral base.

The frustrations of the Republican Party coincided with the frustrations of social conservatives, many of them located in the South. Trends in social behavior were troubling social conservatives, Republicans were sympathetic, and there were possibilities to increase their electoral support in the South. Beginning in the 1960s, a number of policies had emerged that troubled conservatives. School prayer had been banned; court decisions required that criminal defendants be read their rights; abortion was declared to be a legal right; and welfare eligibility standards were eased and the numbers receiving aid increased significantly. Coinciding with these decisions, crime rates increased, illegitimate births began a steady rise, and divorce became more common. Depictions of sex and sexual themes on television increased.[24]

Those who believed strongly in traditional morals and standards of behavior were troubled by these decisions and trends. Their sense was that government was condoning, approving, and even supporting these changes. They wanted government to play the role of reestablishing traditional norms by reinstating school prayer, limiting criminal rights, banning abortion, limiting access to welfare, making divorce difficult, and limiting sex on television. Government could play a role in establishing an environment to encourage the proper individual behavior.[25]

The emergence of these concerns presented an opportunity and a gamble for Republicans. Despite their gains in the South, by 1990, the party was winning only 34 percent of the seats in the South, whereas their success in the Northeast was gradually but steadily eroding. If the party was going to become the majority party, it needed to increase its success, and it appeared that its best prospects were in the South. The social conservatives presented

[24] For a review of all these changes, see Mark D. Brewer and Jeffrey M. Stonecash, *Split*, Chapter 6.
[25] James D. Hunter, *Culture Wars: The Struggle to Define America* (New York: Basic Books, 1991); James D. Hunter and Alan Wolfe, *Is There a Cultural War?* (Washington, DC: The Brookings Institution, 2006); and McGirr, *Suburban Warriors*.

an important possibility and many of them were in the South. A focus on their concerns could win southern votes.

However, that focus represented a significant gamble. Many social conservatives were motivated by fundamentalist religious views based on some enduring moral codes. Appealing to social conservatives with religiously based language would appeal to many southerners, because religion was much more important to voters in that region than elsewhere. However, religion was far less important in the daily lives of individuals in the Northeast, partly due to the rising proportion of Americans who did not identify with any religion at all. One recent survey, for example, found that the proportion of nonidentifiers in the Northeast, rose from 7 percent in 1990 to 17 percent in 2008, a higher increase than in any other region.[26] Too clear an identification with southern fundamentalists could hurt elsewhere. Other social conservatives were not religious but were motivated by a strong sense that traditional values and authority structures should be adhered to. The presence of those with authoritarian beliefs was also greater in the South and less prevalent in the Northeast, where many Catholics and Jews, so numerous in the region, were uncomfortable with the moralism of fundamentalists. Appealing to authoritarian beliefs could also cost the party in the Northeast. [27]

The larger dilemma was mixing an antigovernment philosophy with one that advocated using government to try to influence social behavior. The issue was whether this combination could work. To some the combination was problematic under the presumption that a commitment to limited government should be consistent.[28] But ideology is a flexible and changing construction of individuals.[29] If Republicans could create a message that

[26] Barry A. Kosmin and Ariela Keysar, *American Religious Identification Survey (ARIS 2008)*. Online at http:www.americanreligionsurvey-aris.org/reports/ARIS_Report_2008.pdf (accessed June 16, 2009).

[27] Hetherington, *Authoritarianism and Polarization in American Politics*, 59.

[28] E. J. Dionne, *They Only Look Dead* (New York: Touchtone Books, 1997).

[29] For an analysis of how party positions can change as social conditions change and politicians adapt, see David Karol, *Party Position Change in American Politics* (New York: Cambridge University Press, 2009).

supported free markets and using government to encourage moral behavior within that context, they could appeal to social conservatives in the South and elsewhere. That would expand their electoral base and attract a constituency more supportive of the developing conservative message of the Republican Party. The gamble was that they would lose those uncomfortable with government trying to influence personal behavior.

In many ways, the decision for the party was an easy one. In the 1980s, Ronald Reagan had sometimes quietly and sometimes not so quietly endorsed conservative moral positions. He spoke of a "culture of life," the phrase that served as a signal to abortion opponents that he supported them. He consistently criticized "welfare queens" and what he saw as immoral behavior. While he was out of office after 1988, the party was steadily moving toward more conservative social policies. The congressional party had more southerners and more social conservatives, which provided a larger base for advocating conservative social positions. Then in 1994, Newt Gingrich and the Republicans surprised everyone by taking over the House of Representatives for the first time in forty years. Majority power made it easier for them to pursue their policy goals and get more attention for those positions.

Over time, the party defined itself as more supportive of conservative social policy. Republicans sought to reinstate school prayer, limit abortion rights, and restrict access to welfare. They opposed equal job rights for homosexuals and proposed constitutional amendments to define marriage as involving only a man and a woman. The result was that the party began to attract more social conservatives. Those who supported those positions increasingly identified with the Republican Party.[30] The party was using moral issues like abortion as a wedge issue to pull more social conservatives away from the Democratic Party.[31] The party was achieving success in responding to social frustrations and taking issues

[30] The specific legislation proposed by Republicans is summarized in Brewer and Stonecash, *Split*, Chapter 6. For evidence indicating the movement of social conservatives and their party identification, see Chapter 7.
[31] Hillygus and Shields, *The Persuadable Voter*, 59–66.

that might previously not been seen as embodying conservative Republican ideas and convincing voters that their party would respond. In doing so, they were getting those voters to define those positions as part of the party's ideology.[32]

THE DEMOCRATS' STRATEGY

For voters during this period, the equally important matter was where the Democratic Party stood on these issues. The party had been engaged in a lengthy internal debate about to how to protect itself from Republican efforts to attract parts of its base.[33] Should the party seek to retain part of its old base, or should it clarify its positions and image with a concern for new constituents? Their debate had ideological, geographic, and tactical dimensions. There were essentially two schools of thought, both of which assumed continued Democratic strength in the Northeast, but which pointed to different sections of the country where the party might be able to expand. Moderates wanted to focus on the South, whereas liberals wanted to stress the same themes used in the Northeast and expand their base to the West.

Buffeted by an almost unbroken string of Republican victories in presidential elections from 1968 through 1988, moderate Democrats in 1985 formed the Democratic Leadership Council (DLC), an organization of office holders and other activists with a decidedly southern tilt and strong business ties.[34] Among its early

---

[32] The process by which these incremental changes have been achieved is analyzed in Thomas M. Carsey and Geoffrey C. Layman, "Changing Sides or Changing Minds? Party Identification and Policy Preferences in the American Electorate," *American Journal of Political Science* 50 (April 2006), 464–477; Geoffrey C. Layman and Thomas M. Carsey, "Party Polarization and Party Structuring of Policy Attitudes: A Comparison of Three NES Panel Studies," *Political Behavior* 24 (September 2002), 199–236; Geoffrey C. Layman and Thomas M. Carsey, "Party Polarization and 'Conflict Extension' in the American Electorate," *American Journal of Political Science* 46 (October 2002), 786–802; and Geoffrey C. Layman, Thomas M. Carsey, and Juliana Menasce Horowitz, "Party Polarization in American Politics: Characteristics, Causes, and Consequences," *Annual Review of Political Science* 9 (2006), 83–110.

[33] For an overview of this debate, see Brewer and Stonecash, *Dynamics of American Political Parties*, 145–165.

[34] On the Democratic Leadership Council, see Jon F. Hale, "The Democratic Leadership Council: Institutionalizing a Party Faction," in Daniel M. Shea and John

members were future presidential and vice-presidential nominees Bill Clinton, Al Gore, and Joe Lieberman. DLC strategists noted that all but one of the Democrats who had won the presidency since 1945 were from southern or border states, and the exception, John F. Kennedy, had a southern running mate. Therefore one of their early strategies was to increase the role of the South in the presidential nominating process by establishing "Super Tuesday," with a large number of southern and border state primaries, in the hopes that this would maximize the chances of a southern nominee such as Al Gore.[35]

This strategy was not simply geographic, however. Because the South was more conservative than the rest of the country, and had in the past been an essential part of the Democratic coalition, another part of the strategy was to have the party move to the center and restore its appeal to white southerners and other "Reagan Democrats." If enough moderates, North and South, could be pried away from the Republicans, the Democrats could again become the majority party. Bill Clinton's victories and Al Gore's popular-vote success in 2000 seemed to ratify the strategy. Skeptics noticed that despite being from the South, Clinton and Gore ran worst in their home regions, but defenders of the strategy argued that nominating southerners was a way to reassure moderate voters around the country that the Democrats were *not* nominating left-wingers who would take permissive stands on social issues.[36]

In contrast, liberal Democrats have argued for a long time that the South is now overwhelmingly Republican. Trying to woo southern conservatives will only dilute the party's message in the

C. Green, eds., *The State of the Parties: The Changing Role of Contemporary American Parties* (Lanham, MD: Rowman & Littlefield Publishers, 1994), 249–250; Hale, "The Making of the New Democrats," *Political Science Quarterly* 110 (Summer 1995), 208–211; and Kenneth S. Baer, *Reinventing Democrats: The Politics of Liberalism from Reagan to Clinton* (Lawrence, KS: University Press of Kansas, 2000).

[35] In 1988, the first year of the southern-oriented Super Tuesday, the strategy backfired. Southern primary victories were split among several candidates, and the nominee that year was Michael Dukakis of Massachusetts.

[36] See also Steve Jarding and Dave "Mudcat" Saunders, *Foxes in the Henhouse* (New York: Simon & Schuster, 2006).

rest of the country and dishearten the Democrats' liberal base. Instead, they argue, Democrats should emphasize social tolerance, a theme that will contrast with Republicans. This will help retain the Northeast and win votes in the Far West, especially the coastal states of California, Oregon, and Washington, but also in swing states like Colorado, Nevada, and New Mexico.[37] As one strategist put it:

> If the Democrats can simultaneously expand and solidify their existing margins of control in the Northeast and Pacific Coast states ... the Democrats can build a national majority with no help from the South in presidential elections and little help from southerners elsewhere down the ballot.[38]

The theme of tolerance would help on the West Coast, where voters tend to be relatively liberal, especially on social issues.[39] Since 1992, every Democratic presidential nominee has carried the three coastal states on the Pacific coast, and the party has made gains in elections on other levels throughout the region.

The way to attract westerners, goes the argument, is to continue to emphasize the party's liberalism, which will not only clarify its image, but also make it more appealing to liberal groups known for their low voter turnout, such as young people and racial minority groups. This brings up a key difference between moderate and liberal strategists, as noted by Thomas Schaller:

> Liberal Democrats tend to favor a *mobilization* (or *base-voter*) strategy, which entails gathering to the polls as many likely voters who are either unregistered or vote sporadically, because when they do turn out they vote reliably Democratic. Centrist Democrats emphasized the need for a *persuasion* (or *swing-voter*)

---

[37] See James MacGregor Burns et al., eds., *The Democrats Must Lead* (Boulder, CO: Westview Press, 1992), especially Jerome M. Mileur, "Dump Dixie – West is Best: The Geography of a Progressive Democracy," 97–111; Arthur Sanders, *Victory: How a Progressive Democratic Party Can Win and Govern* (Armonk, NY: M. E. Sharpe, 1992); and Thomas F. Schaller, *Whistling Past Dixie* (New York: Simon & Schuster, 2006).

[38] Schaller, *Whistling Past Dixie*, 3.

[39] C. B. Holman, "Go West, Young Democrat," *Polity* 22 (1989), 323–339.

strategy, in which uncommitted moderates and independents from among the pool of reliable voters are contacted in an effort to convert them to Democratic votes.[40]

The mobilization strategy favored by liberals is reminiscent of the argument made by E. E. Schattschneider many decades ago that an important determinant of the outcome of a political struggle is the scope of the conflict or the number of participants.[41] In this example, bringing nonvoters to the polls would be a more effective way to win than trying to woo voters who already lean Republican. This approach also brings to mind the 1980s strategy of presidential candidate Jesse Jackson, who inspired numerous African Americans to register and vote for his leftist campaign, and the more successful candidacy of Barack Obama in 2008, whose campaign substantially increased the turnout of young people and blacks.

In the end, Democrats tried both strategies, often simultaneously. All of the national tickets from 1988 through 2004 included a southerner, and most entailed attempts to avoid being identified with liberalism of the sort associated with George McGovern's failed campaign of 1972.[42] At the same time, substantial Democratic resources were devoted to building the party in the West, notably in national chair Howard Dean's "fifty-state strategy" after 2004.[43] In this regard, Obama achieved success in both worlds in November 2008: He carried seven western and three southern states.

Ultimately, though, a party's image is not merely the result of its presidential campaign. Democrats in Congress, like their Republican counterparts, are a more ideological group than their presidential nominees. For Democrats, this has resulted in the fact that more than 60 percent of Senators and Representatives

[40] Schaller, *Whistling Past Dixie*, 174; emphasis in the original.
[41] E. E. Schattschneider, *The Semisovereign People: A Realist's View of Democracy in America* (Hinsdale, IL: Dryden Press, 1960).
[42] See Bruce Miroff, *The Liberals' Moment: The McGovern Insurgency and the Identity Crisis of the Democratic Party* (Lawrence, KS: University Press of Kansas, 2007).
[43] See Matt Bai, *The Argument: Inside the Battle to Remake Democratic Politics* (New York: Penguin, 2007).

from the Far West, including Senate Majority Leader Harry Reid and Speaker Nancy Pelosi, are Democrats, compared with fewer than half of southern Senators and Representatives. The tendency of these western Democrats has been to emphasize tolerance on social issues. Their behavior contributes to a national image that is more appealing to northeasterners.

THE REPUBLICAN PURSUIT OF VOTERS: GAINS AND LOSSES

The result of these party developments was that party images were diverging.[44] Republicans were creating an identity as the party more responsive to social conservatives, which was likely to alienate those supportive of culturally liberal positions. The issue again was whether the Northeast differed from the rest of the nation such that its reaction would be different. If the party was pursuing one constituency, was it at risk of losing another? The abortion issue, which has come to embody the disagreements on social issues between the two parties, provides a way to assess what the pursuit of social conservatives did to the Republican Party in the Northeast. The issue draws intense reactions among many, so how the party stance has been received is important.

First, there is the issue of how opinions on the issue vary by region. Voters have been asked since 1972 about their opinions on the abortion issue. They are presented with four positions: abortion should never be allowed; it should be allowed only in cases of rape, incest, and to protect the health of the mother; it should generally be allowed with some restrictions; or, it should always be available. To simplify, the first two are regarded as pro-life and the latter two as pro-choice.

Figure 6.3 indicates how support for the pro-choice position has varied by region over time. The Northeast has been slightly more pro-choice than the rest of the nation since the question was first

---

[44] Jeffrey M. Stonecash, Mark D. Brewer, and Mack Mariani, *Diverging Parties: Social Change, Realignment, and Party Polarization*, (Boulder, CO: Westview Press, 2003).

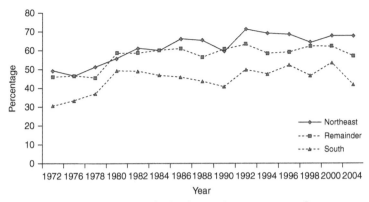

Figure 6.3. Percentage pro-choice by region, 1972–2008.

asked. Most importantly, the Northeast has moved steadily more pro-choice over time. By the 2000s, almost 70 percent chose that position in surveys. The South has been more divided, with 50 percent or less choosing that position, and the remainder of the nation generally falls in between the Northeast and the South.

At the same time that the Northeast's population was becoming more pro-choice than the rest of the nation, the issue was becoming more divisive nationally. As many have noted, opinions about abortion did not create partisan divisions in the 1970s and for most of the 1980s. While the *Roe v. Wade* decision was made in 1973, politicians over the next decade or so were still unsure about how to respond to the groups on either side of the issue. Gradually Republicans concluded that they could use abortion as a wedge issue to attract social conservatives.[45] The party began to make its support for the pro-life position known whereas Democrats were making their support for the pro-choice position clearer, and voters began to see the difference.[46]

The strategy worked, and the Republican Party attracted those who supported using government to limit access to abortion to the

[45] Karol, *Party Position Change in American Politics*; Kira Sanbonmatsu, *Democrats, Republicans, and the Politics of Women's Place* (Ann Arbor, MI: University of Michigan Press, 2002).

[46] Brewer and Stonecash, *Split*, Chapters 6 and 7.

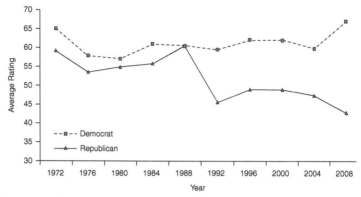

Figure 6.4. Rating of Republican and Democratic parties by those pro-choice, Northeast only, 1972–2008.

party. There was also a cost to the strategy. The Republican Party was pursuing a position that was in a distinct minority within the Northeast. That position was affecting reactions to the party.[47] For some time, the National Election Studies have asked voters about their general reactions to the political parties. Voters are asked to rate the parties on a scale from 1 to 100, with less than 50 being "cool," 50 being neutral, and greater than 50 being "warm." Figure 6.4 indicates how average ratings of the two parties have varied over time within the Northeast for those who are pro-choice. From 1972 through 1988, differences in opinion about abortion produced only a modest difference in the rating given the two parties. Republicans received only a slightly lower rating. From 1992 on, the difference increased because the average rating given Republicans dropped below 50. Within the Northeast, the Republican Party was facing a situation in which 70 percent of voters were pro-choice and much more favorable to the Democratic Party.

Staking out the pro-life position eventually helped the party among those supportive of that position. From 1980 through 1996,

---

[47] Borick's analysis of defectors from the Republican Party in Pennsylvania indicates that 67 percent of defectors were pro-choice and 19 percent were pro-life. See "Where Have All the Republicans Gone? An Examination of the Causes of the Demise of Republican Party Registration."

there was little difference in the rating of the two parties among those pro-life. By 2000, Republicans had a slight advantage (60.4 to 57.8) and by 2004, the advantage was 64.1 for Republicans to 48.8 for Democrats. This gain was more than offset by the fact that most voters were pro-choice. Pursuing this issue brought them some voters but cost them others.[48]

Much less of a difference has developed within the South. The evaluations of the Republican Party by those pro-life and pro-choice remained in the upper 50s or low 60s. In the remainder of the nation, the pattern looks much like that in Figure 6.4, but with a smaller percentage in the pro-choice category.

The Republican Party was staking out an identity as the party more committed to traditional morals. It was identifying itself more with those with a strong attachment to religion.[49] It was more supportive of prayer in school. Its leaders spoke about the importance of religion more than Democratic leaders did. Moving to a pro-life position was part of this general emphasis on religion. The shifts the party was undergoing were working to attract those targeted. Those pro-life, those who were more attached to religion, who attended church more, and who relied on religion for guidance were moving to the Republican Party.[50] The party's strategy was working.

The difficulty for the party was that the population within the Northeast was less committed to religion and did not react favorably to this emphasis. There are multiple indicators that might be

---

[48] There was also a significant shift in public opinion on another cultural matter – tolerance or acceptance of homosexuals. In 1984, the first year the rating question was asked, within the Northeast the percentage of those above 50 years of age tolerant to homosexuals was 18.8. By 2004, it was 45.0. Within the South, the change was from 8.4 to 23.7, whereas in the remainder of the nation, the change was from 12.7 to 34.5 percent. The Northeast was more accepting of homosexuals. While that difference existed, those below 50, at 50, and above 50 already had developed differences in ratings of the parties by 1984, and those differences stayed fairly stable. Among those under 50, Democrats were generally rated a few points less than Republicans, while among those over 50, Democrats were rated 10 to 19 points less, and those differences were stable. With more voters moving into the above-50 category, this shift added to the net positive rating of Democrats from 1984 to 2008.

[49] Brewer and Stonecash, *Split*, Chapter 6.

[50] Brewer and Stonecash, *Split*, Chapter 7.

used to capture the relevance of religion to people, but perhaps the most direct one is that which asks voters about the importance of religion in their life. Specifically, the question is "How important is religion in providing guidance in your life: some, quite a bit, a great deal, or religion is not important." Table 6.8 first presents the percentage choosing each response by region. Then the percentage within each of those groups that indicates they identify with the Republican Party is shown to the right. At the bottom of each region is shown the change from the 1980s through the 2000s in either the percentage indicating the importance of religion, or the percentage identifying with the Republican Party.[51] Among the seculars, there was an increase in Democratic Party identification.

The Northeast and the remainder of the nation differ significantly from the South in the importance of religion in people's lives. In the South, almost 50 percent consistently say that religion matters a great deal in their lives. Outside the South, only half that percentage says that. The emphasis of the Republican Party on religious themes was successful in the South because voters in that region were much more predisposed to respond to that focus. It also meant, however, that the Republican Party was creating an image not likely to be well received in the Northeast. The right half of Table 6.8 indicates how identification with the Republican Party changed over time by the importance of religion. Those in the Northeast who did not see religion as important reacted the most negatively, dropping almost 11 percentage points in their identification with the party. Below the net change in Republican Party identification is the net change in Democratic Party identification. Over the three decades in the Northeast, the percentage of those who regard religion as not important moved Democratic by 19.5 percentage points.

As with issues of race, ideology, and abortion, the Northeast differs from the rest of the nation, and particularly the South. Voters in the Northeast are less likely to be conservative, and as

---

[51] The responses are from the NES cumulative file and the 2008 NES survey.

TABLE 6.8. *Importance of religion and Republican Party identification by region, 1980s–2000s*

Decade	Distribution of Responses				Republican Identification Within Groups			
	Not import	Some	Quite a bit	Great deal	Not import	Some	Quite a bit	Great deal
Northeast								
1980s	26.0	22.8	24.1	27.0	38.4	41.1	42.2	43.0
1990s	26.6	22.7	21.9	28.8	35.4	32.8	33.0	37.4
2000s	31.6	20.7	19.3	28.5	27.9	42.0	39.1	42.6
Δ 1980s–2000s	+5.6	−2.1	−4.8	+1.5	−10.5	+.9	−3.1	−.4
South								
1980s	12.3	17.6	21.5	48.6	35.9	32.0	32.3	28.7
1990s	12.5	14.3	23.6	49.6	36.9	34.7	40.1	30.8
2000s	12.8	13.6	22.8	50.8	51.3	42.0	46.5	43.0
Δ 1980s–2000s	+0.3	−4.0	+1.3	+2.2	+15.4	+10.0	+14.2	+14.3
Remainder								
1980s	24.1	27.5	24.0	24.4	34.8	40.6	43.1	46.6
1990s	34.4	16.1	24.2	25.2	33.6	38.8	44.4	53.1
2000s	33.0	15.4	27.4	24.2	34.7	37.7	42.2	50.7
Δ 1980s–2000s	+8.9	−12.1	+3.4	+0.3	−.1	−3.9	−0.9	+4.1

the Republican Party has become more conservative, the party has alienated those in the Northeast who are not conservative.

The problem for the party in the Northeast goes beyond just adopting conservative positions. The Republican message in the last several decades has had a populist thread to it, a sense that the values of the common man have been neglected and not respected.[52] The party has argued that enduring and simple values should be honored. The world is not complex and behavior can be based on those simple values. That stance conflicts with many of those who have pursued higher education and believe in careful analysis of issues and expertise. The stance largely embraces absolute values and rejects the value of analysis. As David Brooks put it in commenting on the candidacy of vice-presidential nominee Sarah Palin during the 2008 presidential campaign:

> [O]ver the last few decades, the Republican Party has driven away people who live in cities, in highly educated regions, and on the coasts. The big [reason] is this: Republican political tacticians decided to mobilize their coalition with a form of social class warfare. Democrats kept nominating coastal pointy-heads like Michael Dukakis so Republicans attacked coastal pointy-heads. The nation [became] divided between the wholesome Joe Sixpacks in the heartland and the oversophisticated, overeducated, oversecularized denizens of the coasts. Republicans developed their own leadership style. If Democratic leaders prized deliberation and self-examination, Republicans would govern from the gut. The Republicans have alienated whole professions. It has lost the educated class by sins of commission – by telling members of that class to go away.[53]

---

[52] Michael Kazin, *The Populist Persuasion* (New York: Basic Books, 1995).
[53] David Brooks, "The Class War Before Palin," *The New York Times* (October 10, 2008), A33. The same point was made by other commentators. Gregory Rodriquez, "The GOP and the Perils of Populism," *Los Angeles Times* (October 13, 2008). At http://www.latimes.com/news/columnists/la-oe-rodriguez13-2008oct13,0,7551792.column; Charlie Cook, "Learn or Languish : The GOP's Focus on Social, Cultural, and Religious Issues Cost its Candidates Dearly Among Upscale Voters," NationalJournal. com (November 15, 2008); Carl Hulse, "G.O.P. Envisions Northeast Comeback," *New York Times* (January 31, 2010), 24.

The difficulty for the Republican Party is that those with higher education are more likely to support civil rights, be more tolerant of diverse values and beliefs, and be more supportive of pro-choice views.[54] Republican positions are likely to alienate those who have higher education and hold those values. This possible alienation of those with higher education has occurred at a time when the percentage of voters defining themselves as professional or upper-middle-class has increased and the percentage of voters with college education or more has been steadily increasing.[55] The important matter is how voters with varying levels of education have reacted to the Republican Party, particularly within the Northeast.

The identification over time with the Republican Party by education level outside the Northeast and within the Northeast are shown in Figures 6.5 and 6.6. Outside the Northeast, the Republicans have consistently done better among those with more education, due at least in part to the fact that highly educated people tend to be wealthier than other people. Since 1952, roughly 50 percent of those with a college education or more have been Republican, whereas those with a high school education or less have remained at about 30 percent. The party has had a relatively stable twenty-point advantage.

Within the Northeast, a different pattern has prevailed. Republicans had a significant advantage from 1952 to 1960 among those with a college degree or more. The nomination of Barry Goldwater resulted in a dramatic drop in Republican identification among those with a college degree or more, from 68 to 42 percent. The drop was not a fluke, as identification remained low among that group, rising briefly in 1984–88 but dropping down again after that. By the 2000s, identification with the Republican Party

54 Matthew E. Wetstein, *Abortion Rates in the United States: The Influence of Opinion and Policy* (Albany, NY: SUNY Press, 1996), 68–69.
55 Mark Penn, "Most Affluent Voters Key to Obama Sweep," Politico (November 11, 2008), http://www.politico.com/news/stories/1108/15471.html; and Alan Abramowitz and Ruy Teixeira, "The Decline of the White Working Class and the Rise of a Mass Upper-Middle Class," in Ruy Teixeira, ed., *Red, Blue & Purple America: The Future of Election Demographics* (Washington, DC: Brookings Institution, 2008).

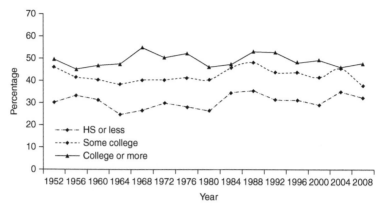

Figure 6.5. Republican Party identification by education level, outside the Northeast, 1952–2008.

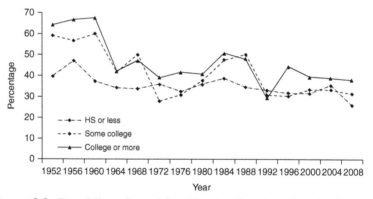

Figure 6.6. Republican Party identification by education level, Northeast, 1952–2008.

among those with a college degree or more was below 40 percent.[56] This group constituted 37 percent of northeastern respondents in 2008 surveys. The identification with the Republican Party among those with a high school degree or less was about the same level as

---

[56] Borick's analysis of defectors from the Republican Party in Pennsylvania indicates that those leaving "tend to be fairly well educated and from middle to upper income categories." See "Where Have All the Republicans Gone? An Examination of the Causes of the Demise of Republican Party Registration."

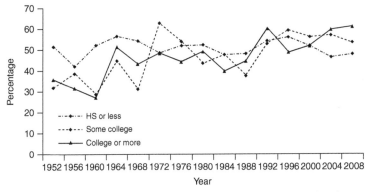

Figure 6.7. Democratic Party identification by education level, Northeast, 1952–2008.

outside the Northeast. The major change was the decline among those with more education.

While Republicans were losing identifiers among those with more education, were these going over to Democrats? Figure 6.7 indicates the percentage identifying with the Democratic Party by education level within the Northeast over time. In the 1950s, the pattern was that those with less education were more Democratic. Then from 1964 to 1988, the pattern became more erratic, largely because those with some college or college or more fluctuated in their identification. Then in 1992, these two groups moved above 50 percent in identifying as Democrats and have largely remained at that level or greater since then. From 2000 onward, those with a college degree or more were more Democratic than those with only a high school degree or less.[57] By 2008, 38 percent of survey respondents within the Northeast said they had a college degree

[57] This might be seen as an example of the "class inversion" that Everett Carll Ladd argued was occurring. See Everett Carll Ladd, "Liberalism Turned Upside Down: The Inversion of the New Deal Order," *Political Science Quarterly* 91, no. 4 (Winter 1976–1977), 577–600. The difficulty is that Ladd proclaimed this to be a national phenomenon in the 1970s, and there was little evidence of that then or in the next decade. See Jeffrey M. Stonecash, *Class and Party in American Politics* (Boulder, CO: Westview, 2000), 73–75. It is also the case, as noted in this chapter and in Figure 6.5, that no inversion occurred outside the Northeast.

or more. This segment of the population was increasing and moving Democratic.

While Republicans were losing those with more education, it is important to note that within the Northeast, the party has not been attracting those with less education.[58] As Figure 6.6 indicates, Republicans have lost ground somewhat among that group within the Northeast. The loss of Republican support in this group has not resulted in an increase in identification with the Democrats (they have stayed at about 50 percent Democratic), but in a significant increase in the percentage saying they are independent. In the NES studies in the 2000s, the percentage of this group regarding themselves as pure independents (those not leaning to either party) has varied between 10 and 26 percent. Where they go in the future depends on the strategies of the parties. As of now, however, within the Northeast, the Republicans are losing those with more education and not attracting those with less education.

This is in contrast with what is occurring elsewhere. In the South, those with more education have moved more Republican, whereas those with less education have remained more Democratic. For example, in 2008 in the South, those with high school education or less were 50 percent Democratic and 34 percent Republican. Those with a college degree or more were 35 percent Democratic and 55 percent Republican. Within the remainder of the nation, there was limited variation by education, with Democrats having a 53–34 percent advantage.

For reasons that are not entirely clear, the Northeast had a more negative reaction to the increased emphasis of the Republican Party on socially conservative positions such as opposition to civil rights, government programs in general, abortion rights, and support for a greater role for religion in society. The more negative reaction is somewhat because of the composition of the Northeast.

[58] The thesis that Republicans have been able to move the less affluent to the Republican Party has been popularized by Thomas Frank, *What's the Matter with Kansas* (New York: Henry Holt Books, 2004). For a critique of that argument, see Larry M. Bartels, "What's the Matter with *What's the Matter with Kansas*," *Quarterly Journal of Political Science* 1 (2006), 201–226.

The population is more liberal, has more individuals with pro-choice views, and is less attached to religion. It is also because those in the Northeast with apparent demographic traits like those elsewhere have reacted more negatively to the evolution of Republican Party positions. Why this is so is difficult to say. It may be because of contagion effects, or the effects of having a greater spatial concentration of those with similar views. Populations that are similar create social norms and exchange views that affect each other.[59] The presence of more people with liberal views within the Northeast may act to create a stronger reinforcement of such views within the region.

Illustrative of the Republicans' problems in the Northeast is their declining ability to mobilize their natural base to identify with the party. In the middle of the nineteenth century, Republicans inherited from the Whig party an affluent, Protestant base. In a word, they have represented the American Establishment, including Wall Street and the broader business community, as well as small-town business owners, from their earliest days as a party. The Republican appeal to such groups was based on several economic and cultural factors.[60] One was a consistently pro-business platform, including sound money, trade protectionism until the mid-twentieth century and free trade thereafter, and general opposition to the regulation of business by the government. Another factor was the alliance of the party with the Protestant clergy, including, at times, fundamentalists; this has made the party more resistant than Democrats to the immigration of non-Protestants and more willing to use the government to promote moral behavior. Partly in response, Roman Catholic voters have always largely identified with Democrats, as have most Jewish voters since the 1930s and other non-Christians in recent years.[61]

[59] Bill Bishop, *The Big Sort: Why Clustering of Like-Minded Americans Is Tearing Us Apart* (New York: Houghton-Mifflin, 2008).
[60] See John Gerring, *Party Ideologies in America, 1828–1996* (New York: Cambridge University Press, 1998).
[61] Clinton Rossiter, *Parties and Politics in America* (Ithaca, NY: Cornell University Press, 1960), 101–102; Milton Viorst, *Fall from Grace: The Republican Party and the Puritan Ethic* (New York: New American Library, 1968), 37; and William E. Gienapp, *The*

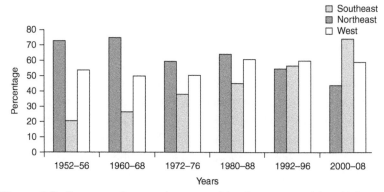

Figure 6.8. Percent of upper-income white Protestants identifying with or leaning to the Republican Party, by section, 1950s to 2000s. *Source*: NES Studies.

Republicans have also been a predominantly white party. Ever since black voters, who had identified with the Republicans since that party was founded as an antislavery party in the 1850s, swung to the Democratic side in the 1930s, Republicans have drawn few members of racial minority groups to their coalition.[62]

And so the Republicans' natural base has long been upper-income (defined as above the median in family income) white Protestants. We can examine the extent to which this group has identified with or leaned toward the party in every decade for which we have reliable survey data.[63] Figure 6.8 shows the results for the Northeast, for the Southeast that has been so distinctive, and for the rest of the country, the Middle West and Far West combined. The dark bars in the graph show that the proportion of northeastern upper-income white Protestants who chose the Republican Party plummeted over the decades, from over 70 percent in the 1950s and 1960s to less than 45 percent in the first decade of the

Origins of the Republican Party 1852–1856 (New York: Oxford University Press, 1987), 434–439.

[62] Paul Frymer, *Uneasy Alliances: Race and Party Competition in America* (Princeton, NJ: Princeton University Press, 1999).

[63] Because of small sample sizes for some of the years, in several of the following tables we have grouped all the years in the same decade.

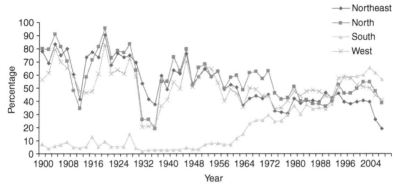

Figure 6.9. Percentage of House seats won by Republicans within regions, 1900–2008.

new century. At the same time, the proportion of such people in the South who chose Republicanism (the gray bars) has skyrocketed; that of westerners (the white bars) has increased only slightly over time.[64]

THE CONSEQUENCES

The process of political change within the Northeast has been lengthy, but it has fundamentally changed partisan outcomes in the region. As noted earlier, Democratic presidential candidates won all states in 2004 and 2008. The partisan outcomes within the Northeast are now very different from the rest of the nation. Figure 6.9 presents House results by region through 2008. By 2004, the party's level of success in the Northeast was less than in all other regions. The problems of the Republican Party in the next four years – the Iraq war and occupation, Hurricane Katrina, and the polarizing effect of George W. Bush[65] – pushed the party

[64] The reader may wonder how the Democrats' natural base behaved. If we define them as lower-income non-Protestants, there was virtually no difference between people who live in the Northeast and those who live elsewhere in their tendency to identify with or lean toward Democrats in any of the decades since 1952.

[65] Gary C. Jacobson, *A Divider, Not a Uniter: George W. Bush and the American People* (New York: Longman, 2007).

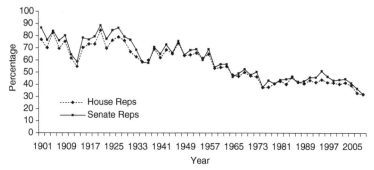

Figure 6.10. Average percentage of seats held by Republicans within the Northeast, state legislatures, 1901–2009.

to an even lower level of success. From 1900 to 2008, the party dropped from winning 80 percent of all Congressional seats to 20 percent. The Republican Party had fallen far.

The decline of the party in state legislatures has been more gradual and has not yet reached the levels of the House; nevertheless, the decline has been relentless, as indicated in Figure 6.10.[66] Following the 2008 elections, the party held an average of 32 percent of seats in state houses and senates. As noted earlier, identification with the party has also declined.

THE FUTURE

The fate of parties is not inevitable. Prior analyses suggest that the Republican Party faces serious problems in the Northeast. It has steadily lost seats, and the negative trends appear to be continuing. The obvious conclusion is that voters have given up on the Republican Party and moved to the Democratic Party, and the Republican Party faces a major challenge in trying to reverse decades of image formation.

---

[66] For an earlier effort to track partisan change in parts of the region, see David R. Mayhew, *Two-Party Competition in the New England States* (Amherst, MA: Bureau of Government Research, University of Massachusetts Amherst, 1967).

There are logical and empirical reasons to be cautious about that conclusion. Parties and their members adjust as they assess their fortunes.[67] Party leaders read election results carefully. They assess where they are winning and where they need to win if they are going to maintain or create a majority. Presidential candidates calculate where they have to win in order to secure a majority of the Electoral College. If the trends are going against them, they do not simply continue with the same themes. Adjustment may take awhile, but no party accepts lengthy minority status without trying to change that outcome. If the Republican Party, or at least some substantial segment of it, concludes that it cannot afford to continue to do so badly in the Northeast and expect to attain a majority, the party will adjust its emphases to try to win votes and seats in the region.

Further there is some evidence that the electorate within the Northeast is not yet willing to fully embrace the Democratic Party. Northeastern residents are voting for Democrats, but there is evidence from some states and from the NES studies that they are not yet willing to fully identify with the party. Most northeastern states provide the option to register and to choose a party when they register. We were able to obtain the complete state file of registrants from several states.[68] The files can be processed in two ways to provide evidence about the likely future of each party within a state. The record for each registrant contains the year the individual last registered and the year of birth. Party choices can be sorted by each – the year of registration or the age of the registrant. The former provides a rough indication of how party choice

---

[67] See David Karol, *Party Position Change in American Politics*; and Brewer and Stonecash, *The Dynamics of American Political Parties* for efforts to explain change with a focus on party adaptability over time.

[68] We could not obtain all of them because some of the states charge a substantial fee to provide the complete file. Connecticut, for example, required a fee of $250. Others were higher, so we declined to request those with high fees. The presumption is that these states are not atypical of changes occurring. The patterns presented here are similar to those reported for earlier years in the collection of state studies in Jerome M. Mileur, *Parties and Politics in the New England States* (Amherst, MA: Polity Publications, 1997).

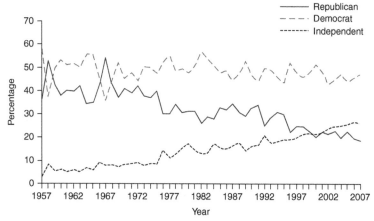

Figure 6.11. New York State party enrollment by year of registration in current BOE files, 1957–2008.

varies by year.[69] The other approach indicates the party choices of older and younger people, regardless of when they most recently registered. For parties, the latter is probably more important. As a population ages and older voters move out of the state or die, the party's fortunes will be determined by the choices of the younger voters.

Nonetheless, the patterns of party choices by year of registration are important. Each state varies in the initial level of choice for each party. Rhode Island has been heavily Democratic for years, so the level of choice for Republicans in the 1960s was already relatively low. New Jersey was more Republican, so levels of choice of the party were high in the 1960s. The general pattern, however, with varying initial levels, is that shown in Figure 6.11 for New York. In

[69] This is not a perfect indicator of party preferences by year. Since many registrants may move over time, their recorded year of registration may be their most recent registration within the state, say 1985, when they really first registered in 1962. If that occurs then many older people, who initially registered 30–40 years ago, are really showing up in the year 1985 or 1995 and, assuming they remain Republican, they are inflating the apparent enrollment in the Republican Party in 1985. While these data are flawed, the basic problem may be that they overstate Republican enrollment in some more recent years. This means that the declines seen could really be worse than it appears.

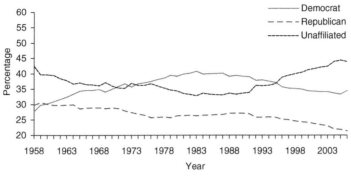

Figure 6.12. Connecticut total enrollment by year, 1958–2007.

the late 1950s and 1960s, the choice of Republican was not much below that of Democrats. Then from the 1960s on, the percentage of registrants choosing the Republican Party steadily declined. The interesting matter is that registration as a Democrat has not increased over time. All the reduction has translated into greater choice for the category of "no-choice" or "blank," referred to as independent in the state. Voters are not choosing the Republican Party but neither are they choosing the Democratic Party at any greater level.

The same pattern has occurred in Rhode Island (not shown). Among those registering in 1950–69, 47.9 percent chose the Democratic Party and 41.8 percent chose "unaffiliated." Among those registering from 2000 to 2008, 40.2 percent chose the Democratic Party and 48.4 percent chose "unaffiliated." The major change over time has been the increase in the percentage of the registrants declining to choose a party.[70]

For other states where individual level data could not be used, the pattern shows up in aggregate enrollment figures. In Connecticut (Figure 6.12) from the 1950s through the mid-1980s, there was an

---

[70] They may still choose to vote Democratic. As Keith et al. document in *The Myth of the Independent Voter* (Berkeley, CA: University of California Press, 1992), most independents lean to and vote for one party. While this is true, the unwillingness to sign up at the local registration office as a Democrat is indicative of the unease about being a Democrat.

TABLE 6.9. *Party registration by age, Rhode Island, New Jersey, and New York, 2008*

Age group	Party Registration		
	Democrat	None	Republican
Rhode Island (n = 673,320)			
18 – 29	36.7	54.4	9.0
30 – 44	38.8	49.1	12.1
45 – 59	41.4	46.9	11.7
60 plus	45.2	43.8	11.0
New Jersey (n = 4,868,338)			
18 – 29	21.0	70.8	8.2
30 – 44	27.5	57.7	14.7
45 – 59	37.2	40.1	22.7
60 plus	43.7	26.8	29.5
New York (n = 11,661,916)			
18 – 29	46.1	27.8	17.6
30 – 44	45.9	22.7	24.1
45 – 59	48.0	18.7	27.6
60 plus	50.2	13.7	32.0

Source: Statewide registration files obtained from each state in 2008.

increase in the percentage choosing the Democratic Party and a decline in the percentage choosing Republican and unaffiliated. Since then, there has been a decline in the percentage choosing either Democrat or Republican, and a steady increase in the overall percentage choosing unaffiliated.

Another indication that voters in the Northeast have not fully embraced the Democratic Party is the pattern of party registration by age. The future of the parties in the region is likely to be significantly affected by the party choices of those currently young. Table 6.9 indicates party choice by age group for three states. In each state, the percentage declining to register with any party is higher among those younger. Younger voters do not appear to

TABLE 6.10. *Party identification, 2000–08, Northeast, by age*

Age group	Party Identification		
	Democrat	Independent	Republican
Initial			
18 – 29	30.0	54.8	15.2
30 – 44	32.3	46.2	21.5
45 – 59	39.1	40.2	20.7
60 plus	30.7	42.2	27.1
All	33.2	45.2	21.5
With Leaners			
18 – 29	60.6	16.8	22.5
30 – 44	49.1	13.1	37.9
45 – 59	58.7	10.0	31.3
60 plus	48.6	10.3	41.1
All	53.7	12.1	34.1

Source: NES Cumulative File, 1948–2004, and the 2008 NES study.

be embracing the Democratic Party. The region may be voting more Democratic, but whether the region is certain to be solidly Democratic is unclear.

Finally this ambivalence is evident in NES surveys that ask about party identification. This question has two parts. Respondents are first asked if the identify as Democrat, Republican, or something else. Those who say they are independent are then asked if they lean to either party. Table 6.10 presents the results for all those within the Northeast in 2000, 2004, and 2008. The percentages are averaged for the three years by age groups to reduce variations across the years and focus on general tendencies.

These results provide further support for the sense that voters have not yet established a clear identification with the Democratic Party. If those who originally say they are independent but are leaning to a party are allocated to that party, it appears that Democrats have a solid advantage within the region overall and

among younger registrants. That identification, however, is not
strong. When initially asked for their party identification, only
33.2 percent of all respondents indicate they identify as Democrat
whereas 45.2 percent say they are independent. Among those
under 30 years of age, 54.8 percent initially chose independent.
Among those aged 30 to 44, 46.2 percent choose that category.
Within those two age groups, more lean to the Democratic Party
than the Republican Party, resulting in a significant Democratic
advantage after leaners are added in. After leaners are added in
among those aged 18 to 29, Democrats have an advantage over
Republicans, 60.6 percent to 22.5 percent. This is heavily influenced by including leaners.

  The point is that among all age groups, Democrats are heavily dependent on leaners to claim a significant advantage in the
Northeast. This is particularly pronounced among those younger.
Republicans have managed to alienate many voters in the Northeast,
but the registration data and party identification responses from
surveys indicate that Democrats have not yet secured a strong
identification with their party. Republicans could yet reverse some
of their fortunes in the Northeast by deemphasizing the cultural
issues that cost them voters within the region. Their reliance on
the South and the opinions that dominate there is significant and
they may not be able to reduce that reliance. Whether or not they
will depends on their calculations of what they must do to be a
majority party.

CHAPTER 7

National Parties and the Position
of the Northeast

There have been remarkable political changes within the nation over time, with the Republican Party coming to dominate the South and Democrats winning most of the Northeast. Republicans are now more conservative and Democrats are more liberal, each party has become more unified within Congress, and there has been an increase in party polarization.[1] We have three concerns in this chapter. First, as changes took place, how have party representatives from the Northeast reacted? Have Republican Members of Congress adapted to their party or to their region? Second, how have these responses affected the national parties? Third, where have all these changes left the region relative to the rest of the nation?

Our focus is first on the voting in Congress, the arena in which members of the national parties assemble for legislative purposes. Congress is a very useful venue for tracking the behavior of regional representatives. It meets every year, it is comprised of members from every state, each party is amply represented in most years in both houses,[2] and the Congress votes on numerous issues of high national importance. We then examine voting at national party conventions.

---

[1] On this last question, see Marc J. Hetherington, "Resurgent Mass Partisanship: The Role of Elite Polarization," *American Political Science Review* 95 (September 2001), 619–631; and Jeffrey M. Stonecash, Mark D. Brewer, and Mack D. Mariani, *Diverging Parties: Social Change, Realignment, and Party Polarization* (Boulder, CO: Westview Press, 2002).

[2] The chief drawback of congressional data, especially for a regionally focused study like this one, is that for long periods, a party may be shut out of particular regions. In the first decade of the twentieth century, for example, there were no Democratic

In answering the questions posed at the beginning of this chapter, we will first show that northeastern members of both parties in Congress were usually more liberal than political actors
from other parts of the country. This fact has in turn has slightly
reduced the degree of polarization in Congress, because northeastern Republicans have not entirely followed their counterparts
elsewhere in the nation.

THE ISSUES THAT REFLECT DIVISIONS

As we examine trends in Congress since the mid-twentieth century, we will be focusing on three sets of domestic issues that have
been the subject of a great deal of public debate and divisions
both between the major parties and within each party. The first
is economic issues, broadly defined. Most of what Congress deals
with involves the role of government in the economy. As James
Madison wrote in the Tenth *Federalist*:

> A landed interest, a manufacturing interest, a mercantile inter-
> est, a moneyed interest, with many lesser interests, grow up of
> necessity in civilized nations, and divide them into different clas-
> ses, actuated by different sentiments and views. The regulation
> of these various and interfering interests forms *the principal task
> of modern legislation*, and involves the spirit of party and faction in
> the necessary and ordinary operations of the government.[3]

The second issue involves race. In the latter part of Franklin
D. Roosevelt's four presidential terms, with a growing civil rights
movement, a deepening divide within the Democratic party
between northern liberals and southern conservatives, and
increasing national embarrassment over the fact that while we

Senators from the Northeast and relatively few in the House (a situation that is not
far different from the predicament of the Republicans today). Until the 1960s, there
were no Republican Senators from the South and rather few southern Republicans
in the House. Such gaps limit our ability to trace certain trends for the whole period
under investigation.

[3] Alexander Hamilton, James Madison, and John Jay, *The Federalist Papers* (New York:
New American Library, 1961), 79; emphasis added.

were fighting racist fascism abroad we were not living up to our highest ideals at home, racial issues began taking their place high on the national agenda.[4] This new cluster of issues such as voting rights for southern blacks and desegregation of public facilities was not as much of a departure from normality as it might appear. While economic issues have always been among the most important and persistent that government has addressed, cultural issues in the form of slavery, prohibition, and immigration have divided people for some time and even led to violence, the Civil War being the most dramatic example.

The final type of issue is far more recent, involving gender. The "second wave" women's movement that grew to prominence around 1970 and the Supreme Court's recognition of abortion rights in 1973 sparked a variety of political issues that have been the focus of some of the sharpest divisions in modern politics. It is fair to say that no Republican politician will be seriously considered for the presidential nomination unless he or she is opposed to abortion, and that no Democrat will be considered who is not in favor of abortion rights.

In each of these policy areas, we review the changes over time in the legislative voting patterns of northeastern Democrats and Republicans, and how they compare with those of other members of their parties. In order to examine voting on economic issues, we take advantage of the DW-Nominate scores compiled by Keith Poole and Howard Rosenthal, who have given each member of Congress a score based on that person's votes on a dimension "that represents conflict over the role of government in the economy," the central political issue throughout so much of American history.[5] We use these scores to compare the voting records of northeastern members of Congress with those of members from

4 See Gunnar Myrdal, *An American Dilemma: The Negro Problem and Modern Democracy* (New York: Harper, 1944); Robert A. Garson, *The Democratic Party and the Politics of Sectionalism, 1941–1948* (Baton Rouge, LA: Louisiana State University Press, 1974); and Kevin J. McMahon, *Reconsidering Roosevelt on Race: How the Presidency Paved the Road to Brown* (Chicago: University of Chicago Press, 2004).

5 Keith T. Poole and Howard Rosenthal, *Congress: A Political-Economic History of Roll Call Voting* (New York: Oxford University Press, 1997), 35.

other parts of the nation. As we shall see, northeastern legislators were frequently the most liberal on the issues involving the role of the government in the economy. However, it is important to remember, as Poole and Rosenthal emphasize, that these scores can be misleading if they are used to compare legislators over broad sweeps of American history, because the issues change dramatically. By confining our analysis to the decades since the New Deal, we are focusing on the period when advocacy of an active role for the government in the economy has meant what we think of as liberal values – social reform, less inequality between classes and races, and vigorous regulation of the private sector. Opposition to such a role has meant conservative values of small government, low taxes, and greater reliance on the private sector for allocation of goods and services.

Since these issues have been central since at least the New Deal, these scores probably represent party unity as much as particular ideologies about the role of the government in the economy. A member of Congress may have voted a certain way less because of firm conviction than due to pressures from party leaders and activists to stick with the party line. Therefore we need to be careful about the precise substantive meaning of these scores. Nevertheless, they are the most comprehensive indicators of voting patterns on economic issues that we have.

As for racial and gender issues, while Poole and Rosenthal calculated scores for a second dimension that incorporated non-economic issues, the content of those issues changed substantially over time and consequently that dimension is harder to interpret. Instead, for racial and gender issues we used the "key votes" selected by the respected journal *Congressional Quarterly* (CQ). Each year the editors choose between ten and twenty votes in each house of Congress that they deem the most important, and we selected from those lists the votes on issues that involved race or gender. Racial issues include, among others, the landmark civil rights laws of the 1950s and 1960s, and later votes on busing and school desegregation. There were thirty-seven votes on racial issues in the Senate (from 1945 through 2007) and thirty-two in the House (1945–2006). Key votes on gender issues mostly involved abortion and related matters, such as the use of discarded fetuses in stem-cell research. There were thirty such CQ key votes in the Senate (1972–2006) and twenty-four House votes (1976–2007).

RESPONSES WITHIN THE NORTHEAST TO CHANGE

How did the behavior of members of Congress change while Democrats and Republicans were trading dominance in the Northeast? While we will analyze both parties, it is the Republicans who are more interesting because they lost much of their popularity in the Northeast while advancing substantially in the rest of the country. Did the remaining northeastern Republican legislators maintain a centrist stance in order to shore up their position in the region, or did they follow their party's national trend and move to the right? We will show that the answer is a little of both. Two matters are important. First, did members from the Northeast within each party move in a more liberal or conservative direction as national change unfolded? Second, how does their behavior compare with the remainder of the party?

We first consider the role of government in the economy. In both houses of Congress, northeastern Republicans have consistently been more supportive of the role of government in the economy than their counterparts elsewhere. Until the 1980s, as Figures 7.1 and 7.2 show, Republicans from the Northeast grew less and less opposed to the role of government in the economy, whereas their fellow partisans from outside the Northeast became gradually more so. Higher positive scores indicate more opposition to a role for government, or a conservative stance. This produced a widening gap between the two groups of Republicans, especially in the Senate where some of the most prominent Republicans – Jacob Javits of New York, Hugh Scott of Pennsylvania, Edward Brooke of Massachusetts, and John Chafee of Rhode Island – were known as leading liberals.

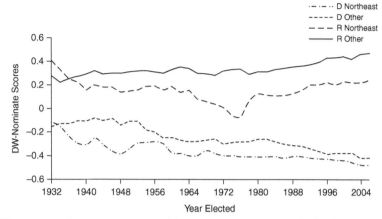

Figure 7.1. Average party position on government role in the economy, by region, U. S. Senate, 1933–2008.

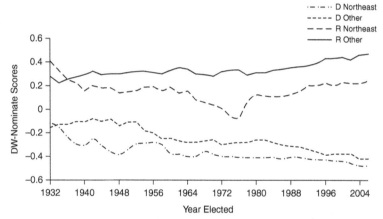

Figure 7.2. Average party position on government role in the economy, by region, U. S. House, 1933–2008.

Then in the 1980s, presumably due to the coming of age of the conservative movement with the presidency of Ronald Reagan, as well as the departure of some of the most prominent northeastern Republican members of Congress, all Republicans began moving away from supporting the role of government in the economy. Despite the change, northeasterners continued to be less opposed to that role than their counterparts elsewhere, especially in the

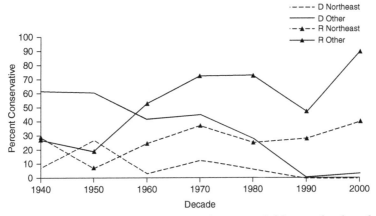

Figure 7.3. Average percent conservative on racial issues, by decade and region, Senate, 1940s–2000s.

Senate. As for Democrats, northeasterners were also consistently less opposed to the role of the government in the economy (more liberal) than fellow partisans from the rest of the country, but over time both group of Democrats moved more toward support for that role, and the difference between Democrats in the two sections narrowed.

The second issue of importance involves race. Figures 7.3 and 7.4 indicate the percentage of Democrats and Republicans from the Northeast and elsewhere who voted conservatively on race legislation from the 1940s through the 2000s. The vote percentages are averaged within each decade to make it easier to see broad patterns, as well as to see and compare party and regional differences.

In the 1940s and 1950s, northeasterners of both parties were less conservative on racial issues than their fellow partisans from the rest of the nation. Republicans in the rest of the nation in those two decades were also less conservative. Democrats from the South stood out in both houses as more conservative. The regional difference within the Democratic Party virtually disappeared by the 1990s, with both groups moving to less conservative positions. This is partly because of the influx of black voters into the Democratic Party in the South as a result of the civil rights

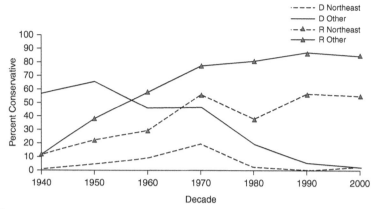

Figure 7.4. Average percent conservative on racial issues, by decade and region, U.S. House, 1940s–2000s.

movement and the Voting Rights Act of 1965, and partly due to the exodus of the most segregationist voters from Democratic to Republican affiliation. The base of the southern Democratic Party became more liberal, especially on racial issues. For example, in 1964, according to the American National Election Studies, fewer than one out of four white southern Democrats supported government actions to ensure school desegregation; by 2000, a clear majority of such Democrats did.

For Republicans, the story was markedly different. Until the 1970s, there was not a wide gap between northeasterners and others of their party. By the 1970s, when Republicans were establishing a *beachhead* in Dixie and the conservative movement was gaining more influence within the party, Republicans outside the Northeast were pulling the party to the right on racial and other social issues. By 1979, Clarke Reed, chairman of the party in Mississippi, said, "There's no ideological contest in the party anymore. We've won that."[6] The result was that in both houses of Congress Republicans in both regions moved in a more conservative direction.

Northeasterners moved rightward in part due to the fact that the issues had shifted from southern segregation to school

[6] Quoted in "Jostling in the GOP," *Newsweek* (May 14, 1979), 38.

desegregation around the nation, and the volatile issue of busing. It has long been observed that on social issues, Representatives tend to be more ideologically extreme than Senators, due in part to the greater internal homogeneity of congressional districts than states. Relatively few House Republicans represent districts with substantial numbers of racial minority groups, while Republican Senators represent states with more diverse populations. Another factor is the greater partisanship in the House, so that on hot-button issues like race, there is more unity around the kinds of party strategies that we have been discussing. Representing fewer African Americans, House Republicans are freer than Senate Republicans to vote against civil rights legislation and play a part in their party's wooing of racial conservatives. The important matter is that northeastern Republicans moved less in a conservative direction than the remainder of the party and are not far away from Democrats.

On gender issues (mostly involving abortion), Figure 7.5 shows that northeastern Democratic Senators were more liberal than other Democratic Senators in the early part of the period, but sectional differences all but disappeared in the 1990s and 2000s. In the House (Figure 7.6), there was never any difference between Democrats from different regions, and they clustered at the liberal end of the spectrum. Republican northeasterners in both houses have consistently been more liberal than other Republicans and have become only somewhat more conservative since the 1970s.

The overarching conclusion is that in recent decades, Democrats have become more unified, whereas the sectional gap among Republicans has persisted. Northeastern Democrats have found themselves squarely within their party's liberal mainstream. Northeastern Republicans, caught between a national party that has shifted to the right and their region that has been increasingly uncomfortable with the more conservative positions of that party, have moved somewhat to the right but not as far as Republicans elsewhere. Nationally and within the Northeast, moderates and liberals have left the Republican Party and conservatives have

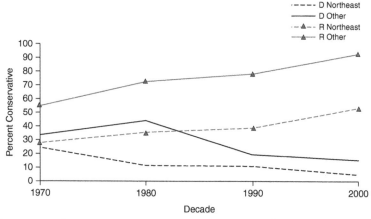

Figure 7.5. Average percent conservative on gender issues, by decade and region, Senate, 1970s–2000s.

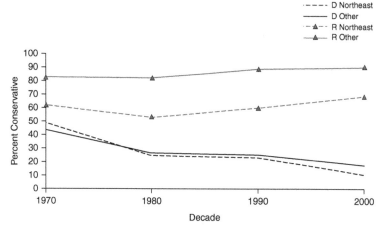

Figure 7.6. Average percent conservative on gender issues, by decade and region, U.S. House, 1970s–2000s.

abandoned the Democratic Party. For northeasterners, usually a relatively liberal wing within each party, all these shifts have meant that Democrats outside the Northeast have "caught up" with them, whereas Republicans outside the Northeast moved farther and farther away from the Northeast. For northeastern Republicans, the way to juggle the conflicting demands of their party leaders and the voters of their region has been to become more conservative, but only within limits.

THE DECLINING LEADERSHIP ROLE OF NORTHEASTERN REPUBLICANS

The shrinking role of northeasterners in the congressional Republican Party has affected their relevance within the party. They are no longer chosen as party leaders. The last northeastern Republican leader in Congress was Senator Hugh Scott of Pennsylvania, who retired in 1976. In recent years, Republican leaders in both houses have hailed from the South and Midwest. It is also the case that Democrats usually select their leaders from outside the Northeast. The last congressional leader from the northeast was Speaker of the House Thomas "Tip" O'Neill of Massachusetts, who retired in 1986. Even if we expand the scope to the entire leadership team, the only northeastern party leader in either party in either house in 2009 was John Larson of Connecticut, chair of the House Democratic Caucus. Perhaps because the Northeast is now regarded as solidly within the Democratic camp, neither party is making a great effort to woo it.

The changes in party success by region has altered the source of committed chairs and ranking minority members, which are largely based on seniority. Figure 7.7 compares the 1961 situation with that in 2009. In both houses, Democrats drew more and more of their committee chairs from the Northeast, especially in the Senate where there were none in 1961. Conversely Republicans drew less and less from the Northeast for their ranking minority members, especially in the House. The increasing ability of northeastern Democrats to get elected and re-elected, and the increasing difficulty of northeastern Republicans to do so, are reflected in these data. In sum, Republicans from the Northeast have become marginalized and Democrats from the Northeast are taking on more committee leadership roles.

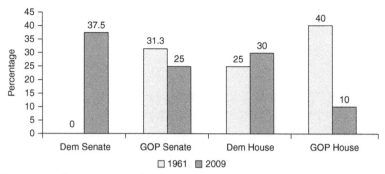

Figure 7.7. Percentage of congressional committee chairs and ranking minority members from the Northeast, by party and House, 1961 and 2009.

THE NORTHEAST IN CONGRESS

The changes within the Northeast have resulted in more Democrats with liberal voting records holding office. As Democrats have become more prevalent, where has this left the Northeast within Congress? With Republicans doing relatively better outside the Northeast, how much does the Northeast now differ from the rest of the nation? We again examine positions on the economy, race, and gender issues. In this case, the analysis focuses on the overall voting record emanating from regions rather than the vote by party.

The voting patterns in the Senate and House by region are presented in Figure 7.8. Higher scores reflect a more conservative position, or opposition to government. Lower scores indicate voting records more supportive of a role for government. Northeastern Senators were quite similar to the other Senators on economic issues until the 1960s. Beginning in the 1960s, however, the Northeast has stood out as the more supportive of a greater role of government in the economy. This trend reinforces our emphasis on that decade as a turning point for the Northeast. Over the next four decades, Senators from outside the Northeast seem to have become more opposed to a government role in the economy, whereas northeasterners have grown decidedly more supportive of that role.

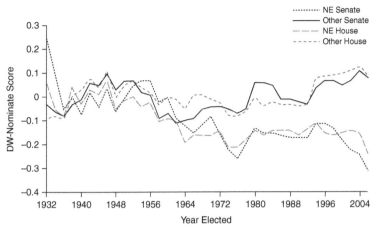

Figure 7.8. House and Senate voting on government role in the economy, by section, 1933–2008.

The trends in the House of Representatives follow the same pattern. Northeasterners were somewhat more pro-government until the 1960s, when the gap between the sections widened. Given that Republicans in both areas were moving to a more conservative position (Figures 7.1 and 7.2), the overall shift of the Northeast to a more liberal position leads us to conclude that the growing proportion of Democratic Representatives within the region has overwhelmed Republican positions and resulted in the sustained movement of the entire region to a more liberal voting record. Both Democrats and Republicans in the Northeast have moved toward greater support for the role of government in the economy, leaving the Northeast more separated from the remainder of the country in voting patterns.

The pattern for racial issues by region and house are shown in Figure 7.9. These data cover the years 1945 through 2007. They represent the same data shown in Figures 7.3 and 7.4, but now organized by region. In the Senate, northeasterners were generally (with the exception of the 1990s) much less conservative than Senators from elsewhere, which is not surprising because "elsewhere" includes the South. Moreover the gap between northeasterners and other Senators remained fairly constant

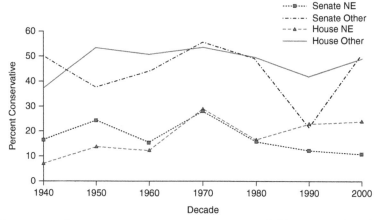

Figure 7.9. Average percent conservative on racial issues, by decade, region, and congressional chamber, 1940s–2000s.

over time. In the House, the regional difference was even more consistent.

The Northeast, unlike with economic issues, did not become more liberal on racial issues over time. Indeed since the 1980s, House members from the Northeast have become somewhat more conservative. That may well be largely due to the fact that racial issues focused less on the segregated South and increasingly more on school desegregation in the North, including the highly charged matter of busing.

Why were the changes in the House so different from those in the Senate? Senate Republicans also moved to the right on racial issues, but to a much lesser extent than their counterparts in the House, and not enough to change the intersectional comparisons shown in Figure 7.9. We noted earlier that on social issues, Representatives tend to be more ideologically extreme than Senators, due in part to the greater internal homogeneity of congressional districts compared to that of states and in part to the greater partisanship in the House.

In the Senate, where northeasterners as a whole moved to the left on racial issues, it was the Democrats who drove that shift. In

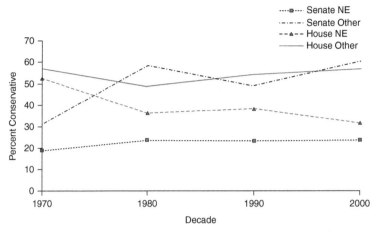

Figure 7.10. Average percent conservative on racial issues, by decade, region, and congressional chamber, 1940s–2000s.

the House, there was a movement to the right, and there it was the Republicans who were responsible for the shift, despite their shrinking numbers in the region. The differing movements of the two parties in each house illustrate the realigning potential of racial issues and indicate that compositional effects were less important than the unique dynamic within each party.

Finally, there is the issue of gender. As shown in Figure 7.10, in the 1970s, regional differences were not clear. Northeastern Senators were the least conservative, but otherwise there was not a clear regional difference. As the subject of the key votes shifted to late-term abortions, the regional difference that was evident on other issues began to emerge. By the 1990s, the gap between the sections widened. The major change was within the House, where northeastern members, increasingly dominated by Democrats, became steadily less conservative. By the 2000s, northeasterners were clearly more liberal than those from the remainder of the nation. Over time, northeasterners became less conservative while others became more so, so the gap between the sections widened substantially.

SUMMARY OF CONGRESSIONAL TRENDS

Our examination of congressional voting patterns indicates several conclusions. First, on economic issues, since the New Deal the Northeast has become the most liberal part of the nation, partly because of growing Democratic success in the region and partly because Democrats have moved to the left on these issues. Second, on racial issues, northeasterners in Congress have been fairly consistently more liberal than those from other parts of the country. Republicans from the Northeast moved to the right during this period and helped reduce the gap between the sections in the House.

Third, on gender issues (primarily abortion) since the 1970s, northeastern members of Congress have again been a relatively liberal group in both houses. Over time, the gap between the sections grew, as members from outside the Northeast grew more conservative and at a faster rate than their counterparts in the Northeast. The growing success of Democrats, especially in the House, helped anchor the Northeast at the liberal end of the spectrum.

Addressing the questions with which we began this chapter, we get a mixed set of answers. Republicans in the Northeast responded to the conservative drift of their party by becoming somewhat more conservative but not as much as the remainder of the party. They adapted to their party and to their region. For all the issues we examined, despite the movement of northeastern Republicans to a somewhat more conservative position, Democrats replaced Republicans, and the overall representation emanating from the region was increasingly liberal. The Northeast now constitutes a distinctly liberal voice within Congress.

POLARIZATION

What role, if any, did these shifts play in the growing polarization between the parties in Congress in recent decades? Here we subtracted the mean Poole/Rosenthal score for Democrats from that for Republicans, as a measure of how far apart the parties were. Including or excluding the Northeast made little difference in any year. In recent years, removing the Northeast would have very slightly increased the polarization between the parties, because northeastern Democrats and Republicans were closer to each other than are Democrats and Republicans in other parts of the country.

Nor did the Northeast affect party polarization on racial or gender issues. In both houses, removing northeasterners would have increased the degree of polarization in most years, because there was less difference between the parties in the Northeast than elsewhere – but not by much. In the House, the Northeast played a more consistent role in reducing polarization on gender issues than it did on any of the other issues; among all Representatives, the mean interparty difference on these issues was 58.6 percent, and with the Northeast removed, it would have been 62.9 percent.

NATIONAL CONVENTIONS

Another way to place the Northeast within the context of national politics is to examine voting at national party conventions. Unlike legislative bodies, conventions are creatures of their parties and include representatives of all state parties that choose to attend the convention. Furthermore, the primary business of the national convention – to select the presidential and vice-presidential ticket, to adopt the platform, and to decide on the rules – includes the most important activities of the national party. Because different conventions have had different numbers of roll-call votes, it would be misleading and unwieldy to examine every such vote. Instead we have selected from each convention a "key vote," usually the decisive vote for the presidential nominee, that indicates the most important division within the convention.[7] Because the

[7] For more details on how these votes were selected, see Howard L. Reiter, "Factional Persistence within Parties in the United States," *Party Politics* 10 (May 2004), 251–271.

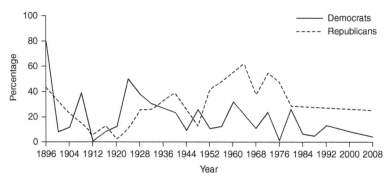

Figure 7.11. Difference between Northeast and other delegations, key votes at national party conventions, 1896–2008.

Republicans had their most recent divided roll-call vote in 1976 and the Democrats in 1992, we have used media reports of how the states were prepared to vote on Ronald Reagan's nomination at the 1980 Republican national convention, as well as delegate counts for both parties' conventions in 2008.[8] Figure 7.11 shows, for each of the conventions since 1896, the absolute value of the difference between how the average northeastern delegation voted and how the average state in the rest of the nation voted.[9] For the Democrats, the Northeast diverged from the rest of the country more before the 1930s than since then, especially in the 1896 convention when William Jennings Bryan's populist appeal fell on deaf ears in the Northeast, in 1908 when the Pennsylvania delegation was the subject of the key vote, and in the 1920s when the ethno-cultural split between northeastern pro-immigrant and anti-prohibition attitudes clashed with the opposite views of southerners and westerners. For the Republicans, northeastern exceptionalism began in earnest in the 1940s and reached its peak with the Goldwater and Reagan candidacies of the 1960s

---

[8] For 1980, see *Congressional Quarterly Weekly Report* (June 28, 1980), 1801; and (July 12, 1980), 1936. For 2008, see http://politics.nytimes.com/election-guide/2008/results/delegates/index.html and http://politics.nytimes.com/election-guide/2008/results/gopdelegates/index.html (both accessed August 16, 2008).

[9] For conventions that had no roll-call votes, we simply connected the line between adjacent points on the graph.

and 1970s. The net effect is that ever since 1952, northeasterners have been far more exceptional among Republicans than among Democrats – a pattern that we have seen in Congress as well.

CONCLUSION

If there is a general conclusion to draw from all of these data sources, it is that the trends we have been discussing had the effect of moving northeastern Democrats farther into the mainstream of their party and northeastern Republicans farther away from theirs. We illustrate this point with all of the measures we have used in this chapter, in Figure 7.12. For this graph, we divided each time period from 1945 onward into two roughly equal periods, calling the earlier one t1 and the later one t2. The exact years varied, as there were different time periods for different measures. For the Poole-Rosenthal economic measure, we multiplied the number by 100 in order for the numbers to be more comparable to the other data.

The first, dark bar in each group of four represents the gap between northeastern Democrats and other Democrats in the earlier period, and the second bar represents the same figure for the second half of the period. In every group except one, the gap between the Northeast and the rest of the country declined from t1 to t2; the only exception was gender votes in the House, where the gap rose only slightly. For Republicans, represented by the last two bars in each group, the gap rose substantially on all measures except, again, gender votes in the House. Without exception, the gap between northeasterners and others in the later period was higher for Republicans than for Democrats.

In short, northeastern Democrats have become more and more like the rest of their party, whereas northeastern Republicans have stood out more and more from other Republicans. Every one of the measures in Figure 7.12 indicates that in the later period, t2, northeastern Democrats were closer to the rest of their party than northeastern Republicans were to theirs; in the earlier period, neither northeastern party was consistently closer to its counterparts elsewhere. These trends reflect the fact that over time, on

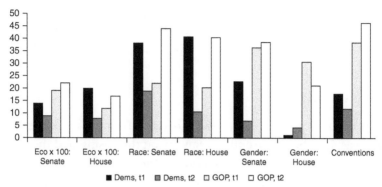

Figure 7.12. Gap between Northeast states and remainder of nation, congressional and national convention votes since 1945.

most issues Democrats across the nation have moved to the left, whereas Republicans moved to the right. This is a consequence of moderates and liberals leaving the Republican Party and conservatives abandoning the Democrats, the process of which we have been discussing throughout this book. For northeasterners, usually a relatively liberal group within each party, this meant that the rest of the Democrats "caught up" with them, while Republicans outside the Northeast moved farther and farther away.

CHAPTER 8

The Process of Change and the Future

Over the past 100 years, the Northeast moved from being reliably and heavily Republican to being a region that Democrats could count on as a source of Electoral College votes and congressional seats. The change was a product of the long-term dynamics of policy positioning between the parties as each sought a majority. The process that created this transition tells us much about how change occurs. This conclusion addresses three questions about change.

First, what creates change, and how does change proceed? Is change a product of abrupt shifts in partisan support because of short-term decisions that parties make, or does it occur gradually as a party repositions itself? Do voters shift their loyalties abruptly or does it take them a long time to recognize and react to a party shift? Second, how much does a party anticipate the consequences of its actions? As a party seeks to pursue an expanded electorate, how well does it recognize the consequences of its shifted emphasis on its ability to retain its older base? Do party strategists misjudge or, as the core of the party switches, is the new core willing to sacrifice the older base in the pursuit of greater party homogeneity and cohesion around principle? Third, to speculate, what are the inclinations and prospects for the party to reverse its fortunes in the Northeast?

THE NATURE OF CHANGE

As often happens in politics, the process of how change occurs is not simple and does not fit one model. There were junctures of

167

significant and relatively abrupt change and eras of more gradual change. From 1900 to 1930, Republicans were safely the majority in the Northeast and despite the large numbers of immigrants entering the region, the party generally declined to support social programs to help newcomers struggling to find jobs. Instead the party stressed that their economic policies created jobs for immigrants and presumed that Democrats, dominated as a party by the South, would not be an attractive alternative. Then the Great Depression occurred, and President Hoover was not inclined to use the federal government's resources to help the unemployed. That prompted enormous numbers of immigrants to vote, and to vote Democratic. Then in 1934 and 1936, Republicans apparently assumed that voters would swing back to their "normal" partisanship within the Northeast, and so the party opposed the New Deal. The choices the party made from 1930 to 1936 cost it dearly. Even in that situation, however, the change was not a clear example of a critical *and* enduring shift from one party to the other. Rather Republicans continually misjudged what the public wanted and engaged in sustained opposition to the New Deal. Once the party accepted the fundamental shift in public support for a greater role for government, some northeastern members shifted to a moderate position, and the party recovered somewhat within the Northeast.

The 1932 election has often been interpreted as a critical – abrupt and enduring – realignment. While there was considerable change within a short period of time, it would be inaccurate to say that the move to Democrats endured in the Northeast from 1932 and thereafter. The change persisted as long as the Republican Party opposed the New Deal. Once they accepted some of it, they regained much but not all of their public support. Republican losses were not enduring but contingent, at least for several decades, on the positions of the party relative to those of Democrats.

By the mid-1940s, the Republican Party had recovered somewhat in the Northeast. It was plausible by then for some to assume that the party's decline within the region was over. But then a period of steady decline within the Northeast ensued. Democrats gradually improved their fortunes in House and Senate seats and party identification. Democrats were pursuing votes in urban districts in the region and making progress. Then an abrupt change occurred with the candidacy of Barry Goldwater. Partisan voting patterns changed significantly in 1964, and Nixon assessed the results and acted on them in 1968 and 1972. Change was again both abrupt and gradual in nature, with the relative policy positions taken by Republican and Democratic presidential candidates crucial to creating a sustained difference.

Since then, the change has been one of steady erosion of the Republican Party's situation. The party was gradually moving to a more conservative position, voters in the Northeast slowly recognized the emphasis on socially conservative positions and the populist dismissal of expertise, and those not socially conservative and with more education moved away from the party.

In short, there have been abrupt drops in support for Republicans, but they were sustained because the party, either through its presidential candidates or Congress, reinforced the altered image of itself. There have also been periods of gradual losses as the image of the party slowly altered. Change occurs in diverse ways, and the actions of both Republicans and Democrats were significant in its facilitation.

ANTICIPATING ELECTORAL LOSSES

Parties seek a majority. When they are in the minority, they must focus on adding new voters to those they have. To add new members, the party must create an image that appeals to voters currently not in the party.[1] In doing so, party leaders may need to consider just how different the new constituency will be from the existing constituency and whether the differences are so significant that they may lose the older base. No party is eager to lose an electoral base if that loss will cost it a majority. As many a politician notes,

---

[1] D. Sunshine Hillygus and Todd G. Shields, *The Persuadable Voter: Wedge Issues in Presidential Campaigns* (Princeton, NJ: Princeton University Press, 2008).

you cannot achieve your policy goals if you are in the minority. For
Republicans, two questions are important: Could they have anticipated the loss of the Northeast and might they have changed the
positions they pursued?

Could Republicans have anticipated the loss of the Northeast?
Were there warnings of trouble and evidence to support those
warnings? As noted earlier, there are many voices and opinions
within a party. Different analysts and commentators offer their
views, and no one is certain how much to rely on various assess-
ments. In the 1950s and 1960s, as noted in Chapter 4, writers in
National Review were certain that the Northeast was unlikely to
embrace Democrats.

However, there were voices within the party that expressed
unease about the direction of the party. During the 1960s, members of the northeastern delegation in Congress expressed their
unease with the emphasis of Goldwater and Nixon on states'
rights and its appeal to southern segregationists.[2] Christian
conservatives began to gain influence within the party in the
1980s, and there has been resistance from moderates since then
to their growing influence.[3] In the 1988 campaign, many objected
to the approach of Lee Atwater and the use of the Willie Horton
ad, which featured a black man leaving prison in a revolving turn-
stile.[4] Northeastern governors like Thomas Kean of New Jersey
argued that the party needed to be more inclusive. He was frustrated that the party had written off minorities, which was hurting
the party in states like his.[5] Another moderate New Jersey governor, Christine Todd Whitman, also argued that the party needed
to be more moderate.[6]

[2] The conflicts surrounding the Goldwater nomination are covered in considerable
detail in Robert D. Novak, *The Agony of the G.O.P., 1964* (New York: Macmillan,
1965).
[3] Clyde Wilcox and Carin Larson, *Onward Christian Soldiers: The Religious Right in
American Politics*, 3rd Ed. (Boulder, CO: Westview Press, 2006)
[4] Eric Alterman, "GOP Chairman Lee Atwater: Playing Hardball," *New York Times*
(April 30, 1989), 30.
[5] Thomas H. Kean, *The Politics of Inclusion* (New York: Free Press, 1988), 240–248.
[6] Linda Feldmann, "A Move to Push Republicans to the Middle," *Christian Science
Monitor* (January 30, 2005). Online at http://www.csmonitor.com/2005/0131/

In the 1990s, unease grew as the party embraced the South, with a more conservative fiscal image going along with social conservatism. After taking over the House of Representatives in the 1994 elections, Newt Gingrich, the Speaker of the House, was convinced that the party had to stake out a clear conservative stance. He led an effort to cut social programs and was willing to shut down government in a confrontation with President Bill Clinton. The moderates within the party were uneasy with the image of shutting down government, a confrontation that cost the party public support.[7] Republicans lost seats in the next few congressional elections, as well as the presidential election of 1996.

For the Northeast, the more significant image change involved social conservatives. As the party attracted more southerners fiscal and social conservatives, stances such as opposition to abortion and gay rights became more prominent. Party members in the North expressed their unease and created organizations to try to portray the party as more diverse. In 1990, the moderates formed the Republicans for Choice and argued that an emphasis on limited government meant that government should stay out of this issue.[8] In the 1990s, Republican moderates in Congress formed the Tuesday Group, indicating the day they would meet to discuss moderate approaches to policy. During the pursuit of impeachment proceedings against Bill Clinton in 1997 and 1998, moderates noted that Democrats and Independents opposed the process[9] and expressed concern about the heavy focus on morality as a basis for proceeding.[10] In 1998, fiscal moderates formed the Main Street

p03s01-uspo.html. In 2005, Whitman published *It's My Party, Too: The Battle for the Heart of the GOP and the Future of America* (New York: Penguin Press, 2005).

[7] David Maraniss and Michael Weisskopf, *"Tell Newt to Shut Up"* (New York: Touchstone, 1996), 84–87.

[8] Robin Toner, "G.O.P. Group Formed to Support Abortion Rights," *New York Times* (April 24, 1990), A21.

[9] Gary C. Jacobson, *A Divider, Not a Uniter: George W. Bush and the American People* (New York: Longman, 2007), 20.

[10] Jill Abramson et al., "Impeachment: The Twists and Turns; How Republican Determination Overcame President's Popularity," *New York Times* (December 21, 1998), A1; and James Dao, "An Immoderate Republican Voice Urges Moderation on Impeachment," *New York Times* (December 13, 1998), A49.

Partnership, devoted to putting the emphasis on fiscal issues. Their membership consisted largely of northern Republicans.[11] As the party moved to make the concerns of social conservatives a bigger part of the party's agenda, there were voices suggesting that the image would cause problems in their states and districts. There was probably no lack of warnings that the party's move to the right would hurt the Northeast's moderate Republicans.

Whether or not the party was warned may not be the issue, however. The more important issue is whether they would have been inclined to change their pursuits. Parties are filled with members who have beliefs and monitor results to see how and where their message is being received. The results of recent decades provided considerable evidence that the party was on the rise. It should not be underestimated how much the feedback from elections was indicating that the message of the party was being well received overall. The party had suffered a gradual decline in its fortunes outside the South, which could be seen as a negative. However, there were also clear signs that the party was making progress. From 1968 to 2004, there were ten presidential elections, and Republicans won seven of them. After years of relying on the Northeast and other northern areas, by the early 1980s, the party was a national party. As Figure 8.1 indicates, after the 1980 election, the party's success rate, while still having some variation, was now more uniform across regions. More and more of their incumbents were in "safe" seats. Their national percentages of seats won in each region were below what they wanted, but they were a national party.

The 1980s were a period of stability, with the party gradually pulling more conservatives to its side. Then in 1994, the party abruptly took control of the House for the first time in forty years and retained it in 1996. In 1994, its success rate varied from 46.1 percent in the Northeast to 57.4 percent in the West. In the next several elections, it continued to win 40 percent of the seats in the Northeast, even as the party pursued a relatively unpopular impeachment of Bill Clinton. The feedback from elections surely

[11] Online at http://www.republicanmainstreet.org/index.php/

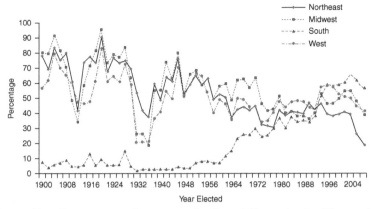

Figure 8.1. Percentage of seats won by Republicans in the House, by region, 1900–2008.

suggested to the party that it was doing well and that it could retain a reasonable number of seats in the Northeast. Then in 2000, the party achieved unified control and did well nationally in 2002.

Perhaps most importantly, the success was seen as a result of a plan. As discussed in prior chapters, the party had first pursued a southern strategy and then made an effort to establish more of a conservative identity. The party had sought to attract fiscal and social conservatives, a strategy that was working. There were more self-identified conservatives than liberals. The party was achieving success, winning 40 percent of seats in the Northeast. Leaders such as Newt Gingrich were convinced that the party was succeeding because it had stopped accommodating the Democratic majority and created a clear alternative. Gingrich had engineered "The Contract with America" and was convinced that providing an alternative was working.[12]

Not only was the feedback from elections positive, but the success of the party was changing its composition and its dominant political ideology was more conservative and more homogeneous. A substantial majority of those identifying as Republican defined themselves as conservative. Republicans not only believed

[12] Maraniss and Weisskopf, *"Tell Newt to Shut Up."*

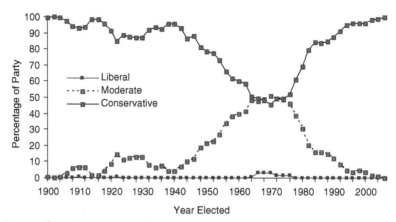

Figure 8.2. Presence of liberals, moderates, and conservatives in the House Republican Party, 1900–2008.

that their plan was working well, but a growing majority within the party believed in what they were doing. The balance within the party was shifting. There was considerable agreement within the party that government was growing too fast, that traditional values were not being honored as they should, and that liberals were dismissive of their concerns. The result of all these matters was that there was less tolerance for moderates. During the 1990s, the term RINO (Republican in Name Only) emerged as a way to characterize those who were not sufficiently committed to the cause.

The combination of increased electoral success and increased dominance of the party by conservatives made the party less receptive to moderates. Figure 8.2 indicates the percentages of the Republican Party in the House who were conservative, moderate, and liberal since 1900.[13] For decades, the party had been dominated by conservatives. Then, as some Republican members of Congress decided to accept much of the New Deal, the presence of moderates increased substantially. Many of these Republican moderates were from the Northeast. As the party began its move

[13] In Figure 8.2, members were classified according to their DW-nominate scores. Those whose scores were .2 or higher were designated conservative, -.2 or less were liberal, and the rest were moderates.

to a more conservative stance during the 1980s, moderates were steadily replaced by conservatives.

Within a remarkably short period of time, moderates almost disappeared. In 1974, 49.7 percent of Republican House members were moderates. By 1984, just a decade later, the percentage was down to 15.9. After the 1994 election, only 5.1 percent were moderates. These distributions are reflections of voting records, so the decline could be because moderates lost and retired or because they were pressured by the party leadership to vote conservatively.[14] Regardless of the reasons, the voting record and tenor of the party were changing, and the electoral success of the party was increasing. The Republican Party by the mid-1990s had become a more homogeneous party, filled with people who believed strongly in conservative principles. They were winning elections and there was little feedback to suggest that the party should not pursue a conservative message.

Furthermore it was not difficult for the party to write off 2006 and 2008 as the result of an unpopular president who badly managed the Iraq War and the response to Hurricane Katrina. Then a recession in mid-2008 further hurt the party. Party members knew that much of the vote for Democrats in those two years could be seen as a vote against George W. Bush. With him gone from the scene, many Republicans could reasonably hope that the underlying support for Republican positions that developed in the 1990s and up through 2006 could return.[15]

There were those within the party who felt that a return to the themes of fiscal restraint and limited government would restore

[14] Barbara Sinclair, *Party Wars* (Norman, OK: University of Oklahoma Press, 2006); John Aldrich and David Rohde, "Consequences of Electoral and Institutional Change: The Evolution of Conditional Party Government in the U.S. House of Representatives," in Jeffrey M. Stonecash, ed., *New Directions in American Political Parties* (New York: Routledge, 2010), 234–250.

[15] Those hopes were supported by evidence that the advantage Democrats had enjoyed in recent years in terms of party identification were eroding in 2009 and 2010. See Jeffrey M. Jones, "More Independents Lean GOP; Party Gap is Smallest Since '05," *Gallup Poll* (September 30, 2009); and Jeffrey M. Jones, "Democratic Support Dips Below Majority Level in 2009," *Gallup Poll* (January 6, 2010). Both reports are available online at www.gallup.com

the attractiveness of the party to those who had left because of the emphasis on social conservatism.[16] By late 2009, the party was seeking seats it might win within the Northeast.[17] The events of 2009 and early 2010 indicated the ambiguity of signs regarding the party's prospects in the Northeast. A 2009 race suggested that getting the national party to accept moderates would not be easy. When in 2009 a Republican House member from upstate New York was selected by President Obama to be Secretary of the Army, a special election was held in November of that year. A state assembly member who supported abortion rights and civil unions for gays was the Republican nominee. The seat had been held by Republicans since 1872. In response to her nomination, the Conservative Party nominated a staunch right-winger, and the Club for Growth, which tries to defeat moderate Republicans in primaries, provided at least $250,000 for that candidate. Perhaps most importantly, the race revealed the ongoing rift within the party. While some within the party were arguing that there needed to be less emphasis on socially conservative positions,[18] the advocates of more conservative positions became involved in working for the Conservative Party candidate, seeing it as "the shot that needs to be fired to Republican leaders." Sarah Palin endorsed the candidate, saying "The Republican Party must stand for something," and the Republican candidate "blurs the lines" between the parties.[19] The Republican nominee dropped out of the race and endorsed the Democratic candidate, who went on to win the seat. That race exemplified the problem that

---

[16] Carl Hulse, "As Republicans Predict a 2010 Surge, Democrats Dig In," *New York Times* (October 10, 2009), A24; Jackie Calmes, "In Saying No, GOP Sees More Pros than Cons," *New York Times* (October 15, 2009), A18; and, Hulse, "G.O.P. Envisions Northeast Comeback," (January 30, 2010).

[17] Raymond Hernandez, "G.O.P. Gearing Up for 2010 House Races," *New York Times* (October 25, 2009), WE1.

[18] Michael Cooper, "Among Republicans, a Debate over the Party's Roadmap Back to Power," *New York Times* (November 17, 2008), A17; and Carl Hulse, "3 Successful Republicans Caution Against a Move to the Right," *New York Times* (November 14, 2008), A33.

[19] Jeremy W. Peters, "Right Takes on G.O.P Choice in a Pivotal Race in New York," *New York Times* (October 27, 2009), A1.

northeastern Republicans have, when the ideological proclivities of Republicans from other parts of the country clash with northeastern sensibilities.

Then in January 2010, a special election was held in Massachusetts to replace Senator Edward Kennedy, who had died in August 2009. Much to the Democrats' surprise, a Republican state senator, Scott Brown, won the seat. It was widely heralded as a sign that Republican fortunes were on the rise.[20] The difficulty was that the meaning of his victory was unclear. Was it an indication of support for a conservative Republican? Or was it a sign that independents in a state with public health insurance, which Brown had voted for, did not want what President Obama and national Democrats were advocating?[21] And how much of Brown's victory was attributable to the ineffective campaign run by his opponent, Attorney General Martha Coakley? As regularly happens in politics, the meaning of the election was unclear, and sorting out what interpretation to accept and act on was not easy. Clearly, the struggle over the future of the party and its prospects in the Northeast will continue.

FUTURE PROSPECTS WITHIN THE NORTHEAST: 2010 AND BEYOND

No party seeks to be in the minority. When electoral returns leave a party in the minority, that party has to reassess why its message is not winning a majority. A lengthy period of time in the minority is likely to prompt even the most ideologically committed to reconsider the party's emphasis.[22] The issue facing the Republican Party in the first decade of the twenty-first century is whether its minority status

[20] Adam Nagourney and Carl Hulse, "Re-energized, G.O.P. Widens Midterm Effort," *New York Times* (January 25, 2010), A1.
[21] Chris Cillizza, "The Importance of Independents," *Washington Post* (January 26, 2010). Online at http://voices.washingtonpost.com/thefix/white-house/the-importance-of-independents.html
[22] Marty Cohen, David Karol, Hans Noel, and John Zaller, *The Party Decides: Presidential Nominations Before and After Reform* (Chicago: University of Chicago Press, 2008), 82–93.

is short lived or long term. If Republicans decide that it is short term and just the result of image problems that will fade as time passes, there will probably be little inclination to change their emphasis.[23] If their status in the minority persists, then they may well have to decide what parts of their emphasis will have to change.

If there is some decision to change their emphasis, the next issue will be whether they need to seek votes and seats in the Northeast or whether they can rely on the continued population expansion outside the Northeast to provide a base for a majority. As of now, the population outside the Northeast is relatively more conservative and may well be more amenable to a conservative message. The party may well decide that its future lies outside the Northeast and that it can proceed without any efforts to support moderates who might win in the Northeast. Given the ideological homogeneity that has developed within the party, that is a proba- ble direction. The western and southern wings of the party have a long history of being uncomfortable with the Northeast, and as the party has shifted its reliance to these other regions, the instinct within the party is unlikely to be to appeal to the Northeast. The very strategy of appealing to the South has put the party in a situ- ation in which moderating its appeal will be less likely.

Still, parties cannot control public policy in the minority. They can have some influence, but it is less. There are trends that suggest that the party may have to adjust. The percentages of immigrants and nonwhites in the nation are growing, and the Republican Party currently does not fare well within these two categories.[24] Many immigrants are settling in the Sunbelt – the South and Southwest – and disrupting the dominance of whites that Republicans have relied on for majorities.[25] As these demographic changes continue

[23] For an overview of that argument, see Mark D. Brewer and Jeffrey M. Stonecash, *The Dynamics of American Political Parties* (New York: Cambridge University Press, 2009), 184–199.

[24] Kerry L. Haynie, "Race and Parties," in Stonecash, ed., *New Directions in Party Politics*, 93–109; and John B. Judis and Ruy Teixeira, *The Emerging Democratic Majority* (New York: Scribner, 2002).

[25] Jane Junn and Marika Dunn, "Immigrants and Political Parties," in Stonecash, ed., *New Directions in Party Politics*, 166–185.

and more immigrants become naturalized and vote, if they remain primarily Democratic, the Republican Party may have little choice but to return to the Northeast to seek votes.

Making an appeal to the Northeast might work if the right set of issues dominates public debate. Beginning with the 2008 slide in the economy, economic issues have become much more salient and have persisted.[26] As the Obama administration has vastly increased federal spending and widened the deficit, Republicans might be able to revive their reputation as fiscal conservatives.[27] They can appeal to fiscal concerns about future taxes and deficits, which are of greater concern to Republicans.[28] The party can also appeal to the interests of the more affluent in opposing changes in health care. Those with higher incomes are much more likely to have health care[29] and to oppose changes in health care.[30] These emphases might help voters, and particularly those in the Northeast, see the party as more focused on older party concerns of limited government and lower taxes, and help the party retain and attract more voters. In this regard, the Tea Party Movement that first arose in 2009, with its focus on traditional GOP priorities of fiscal conservatism and limited government, may help the party in the Northeast.

Making such a shift in emphasis, however, will not be easy. In the last several decades, the Republican Party has steadily and successfully sought to attract social conservatives.[31] The base of the party is now largely outside of the Northeast and is heavily

[26] Peter S. Goodman, "Millions of Unemployed Face Years without Jobs," *New York Times* (February 20, 2010), A1.

[27] Mark A. Smith, *The Right Talk* (Princeton, NJ: Princeton University Press), 178–202.

[28] Frank Newport, "Sharp Differences in Partisan Views of Economic Problems," *Gallup Poll* (June 26, 2009). Online at http://www.gallup.com/poll/121262/Sharp-Differences-Partisan-Views-Economic-Problems.aspx

[29] Frank Newport, "Health Insurance Coverage Varies Widely by Age and Income," *Gallup Poll* (February 22, 2010). Online at http://www.gallup.com/poll/126143/Health-Insurance-Coverage-Varies-Widely-Age-Income.aspx

[30] David W. Brady and Daniel P. Kessler, "Who Supports Health Care Reform," *P.S.* 43, no. 1 (January, 2010), 1–5.

[31] Laura A. Olson, "Religion, Moralism, and the Cultural Wars: Competing Moral Visions," in Stonecash, ed., *New Directions in Party Politics*, 148–165.

conservative and religious.[32] This base is not likely to be pleased
by a de-emphasis on the concerns that are most salient to them. A
move away from social conservatism could cost the party enthusi-
astic support, donations, and party workers from that base. This
base now dominates the party's presidential primary nomination
process, and ignoring it will be very difficult for candidates. Given
the likely dominance of economic issues in the early 2010s, the
party may be able to emphasize economic issues and do better in
the Northeast, but economic issues may not persist in prominence,
and social conservatives will not surrender their influence eas-
ily. Leaders like Sarah Palin, Minnesota governor Tim Pawlenty,
and former Arkansas governor Mike Huckabee have based their
appeal to a great extent on social issues.

There is, of course, no way to predict what trends will continue,
what direction the Republican Party will choose, and how it will
fare in the Northeast in the future. We can only wait and watch
in that regard. What is clear is that the party did engage in a long
process of assessment and strategy that brought it to a point where
its support in the Northeast has badly eroded. It will be difficult to
regain in the short term.

[32] Frank Newport, "Republican Base Heavily White, Conservative, Religious," *Gallup Poll* (June 1, 2009). Online at http://www.gallup.com/poll/118937/Republican-Base-Heavily-White-Conservative-Religious.aspx

Index

For EU product safety concerns, contact us at Calle de José Abascal, 56–1°,
28003 Madrid, Spain or eugpsr@cambridge.org.